Praise for

Noelle strengthened my spiritual core while providing the fitness and nutritional framework that led to my 40-pound weight loss. She taught me to give my best in all situations, forgive my imperfections and focus on what I can control: myself. Noelle helped me set goals, dream big and she held me still long enough to so I could realize my self-worth.

—**Margarita Salgado**, Engineering Change Analyst and *Transformation by Truth* Boot Camp Athlete

When I read Noelle's book, I found myself laughing at her stories because I can relate to them. Noelle puts her heart into all she does and she sees the gifts in each one of us. She motivates and inspires me to dream big and believe in myself. This book will change your life.

—**Jill Turner**, Acupuncturist/Massage Therapist and *Transformation by Truth* Boot Camp Athlete

Filled with living examples of how to transform your heart, mind, soul and body, Noelle's book is a must read for all those looking for long-lasting life changes.

—**Audry Murr** Full-time Mom and *Transformation by Truth* Boot Camp Athlete

Noelle makes it her business to not only change your body, but to inspire you to reach your highest potential with your heart, body and mind. This experience will truly transform you. We highly recommend it to anyone we meet.
> —**Bill Dunn**, Franchise Developer and *Transformation by Truth* Boot Camp Athlete
> —**Holly Dunn**, Controller and *Transformation by Truth* Boot Camp Athlete

Noelle's techniques are beautifully complemented by her heart and spirit-filled dedication. Through her guidance, I've found much peace, joy and a deepened spirituality which has brought me to my ultimate dream life: I am 29 pounds lighter; my mind defaults to optimism; and I have an intimate relationship with God. I am the person I always wished I could be!
> —**Robin Scruggs**, Human Resource Analyst and *Transformation by Truth* Boot Camp Athlete

Noelle's unique leadership inspires others to dream more, do more and become more.
> —**Pamela Wasley**, CEO of Cerius Interim Executive Solutions and *Transformation by Truth* Boot Camp Athlete

Because Noelle believes in your mind being as fit and healthy as your body, her workouts incorporate life coaching techniques as well as challenging, creative and fun physical activities. I have become more self-confident and happy with myself as I work with her. As you read the stories in this book, Noelle's passion for life, love of people and the ability to find humor in almost any situation is the common thread weaving through them.
> —**Dianne Hansen**, Retired Teacher and *Transformation by Truth* Boot Camp Athlete

Transformation by Truth

30 DAYS TO A HEALTHY HEART, MIND AND BODY

Noelle Dey

Copyright © 2012 Noelle Dey

All rights reserved. No portion of this work may be reproduced or transmitted in any form or by any means, electronic or mechanical, including photocopying and recording, or by any information storage and retrieval system, without prior written permission from the author.

If you want to share your transformative stories after trying this 30-day program, email Noelle at: 30days@transformationbytruth.com

Scripture quotations in this publication are taken primarily from:

The Holy Bible, New International Version®. Copyright © 1973, 1978, 1984 Biblica Inc™. All rights reserved worldwide. "NIV" and "New International Version" are trademarks registered in the United States Patent and Trademark Office by Biblica, Inc. ™.

Some Scripture quotations are also taken from:

The New King James Version. Copyright © 1982 by Thomas Nelson, Inc. Used by permission. All rights reserved.

The lyrics on page 132–133 are from:
"I Hope You Dance"
Words and Music by Tia Sillers and Mark D. Sanders. Copyright © 2000 Sony/ATV Music Publishing LLC, Choice is Tragic Music, Universal Music Corp. and Soda Creek Songs.
All Rights on behalf of Sony/ATV Music Publishing LLC and Choice is Tragic Music administered by Sony/ATV Music Publishing LLC, 8 Music Square West, Nashville, TN 37203. All rights reserved. Used by permission. All Rights on behalf of Soda Creek Songs controlled and administered by Universal Music Corp. International. Copyright secured. All rights reserved. Reprinted by permission of Hal Leonard Corporation.

The citation on pages 57-58 is from:
Waking the Dead by John Eldredge. (Nashville: Thomas Nelson, 2006). Used by permission.

ISBN: 1466205407
ISBN-13: 9781466205406

To Ryan… the love of my life. God has worked miracles through you to transform my world. I hope to take the immeasurable gifts you've given me and share them with others.

To our beautiful Sierra… May you always be deeply rooted in God's unending love. You are fearfully and wonderfully made. Daddy and I marvel at the gift of being your parents. We love you honey.

Acknowledgements:

Ryan, there are no words to adequately express my immense love and gratitude for you. I never even knew what a "Malachi blessing" was before you wonderfully crashed my world. The fact I'm your wife is proof positive of God's abundant grace because there's nothing I could have possibly done to deserve the gift of YOU in my life. You are a treasure… my God-seeking, edgy warrior… I love you more than you can ever imagine!

Sierra, you are the main reason this book was written. Not only do I want my love for you to be evident in these words, but I also want you to see that your Mommy is a goof ball. I pray that you can see beauty in all the mistakes I've made in my life. My shortcomings are proof that you never have to strive for perfection—Daddy and I don't expect or desire that of you. You are a gift because you are you. Period. Case closed. I hope you enjoy the timeless truths of God's words through these stories.

Lori, there hasn't been a single day of my life when you weren't there. You have been my confidante and my encourager. Thank you for being there to celebrate my greatest joys and to listen to my biggest frustrations. You're the only person who knows as much *Brady Bunch* trivia as I do and you are one of a very select group that knows the song "Run Joey Run" (just us and the Nittas). I guess what I'm trying to say is, you're cooler than cool and I am humbled that God would give me the gift of you as my sis. I will not cease in praying for your full and complete healing from PLD. Dave, thank you for being the most amazing husband to Lor and for being my big bro.

Mom and Dad, it's hard to comprehend that I really will get to see you… laugh with you… share with you…live with you… again. I can see Mom dancing to the mariachi music, telling the angels that she is "Mexicanese"… and I'm sure Dad is having the heavenly marching bands play the UCLA fight song. I am so proud to be your daughter. Heaven is blessed to have you two.

The Dey Family, did you know that I swore up and down I was never going to let go of my maiden name? That was… until I met Ryan and each of you. The moment I did, I wanted nothing more than to be a Dey. I love my crazy family!

Don… DJ my man… I am praying (in Jesus' name, buh-bye) that this book is evidence of your relentless belief in me. Thank you for being my pastor and my friend. I have immense gratitude for the numerous hours you spent counseling and mentoring me.

Billie, do you remember that initial conversation way back when? Here's to grass roots efforts, baby! Thank you for your friendship and for your heart to get God's truth out to a hurting world. The encouragement and wisdom you have given to me took my writing from a little Word document to what it is now. Thank you!

When I say "fierce," our boot camp team thinks of the one and only Rebecca Johnson. Not only have you inspired our team with your 160-pound weight loss, but you have brought me to new levels of determination, hysterical laughter, and the deep desire to be an excellent trainer. I knew you were a great writer and editor, but I had no idea I would be on the receiving end of your editing talents. This, along with your genuine friendship, is a gift I'll treasure for a lifetime.

Acknowledgements:

Hollywood, you personify grace under fire. Thank you for bringing the truest friendship to my life. With our alter egos MC and K2, we will continue to journey these roads in search of cures for FAP patients... especially for numbers 20 and 21! Thank you and Wayne for the amazing gift of Brian Maul's talents and his patience with my rapid-fire scatter-brained thoughts.

Jill "Geo," Karen, Erika and Dr. Ray, thank you for your friendship and for keeping my body in working order so I can continue to sprint up hills.

Heather, I am so grateful to have a little sis to walk these life roads with. Thank you for the coolest logo I've ever seen. You are brilliantly creative, a genuine friend, a talented boot camp instructor and you keep me laughing with your one-of-a-kind stories.

Greg-who-is-not-Asian-Lee, isn't it funny how you thought boot camp meant that I would be the one helping you? I'm sure you didn't intend to be my all-things-writing expert, but thank you for accepting the role! You are an incredible talent and a good man.

To my amazing team of boot camp athletes who I have the privilege of working out with at o'dark thirty... you have taught me endless life lessons. I hope to give back to you as you have generously given to me.

I remember praying for faith-filled girlfriends *years* ago. Little did I know that God would generously honor my long forgotten prayers which I had abandoned. My life is so rich being a part of "Girls for God" and the Philippians 4:6 prayer warriors. Cute girls, thank you for your unconditional support, your intercessory prayers, and the silly laughter that can only come from girlfriends.

Introduction

Have you tried every diet and exercise gimmick only to find the weight you lose somehow finds its way back home to your belly or hips? When the New Year rolls around, do you resolve to read the Bible each morning yet still feel disconnected from God? When you draw a line in the sand saying that you're going to be a "glass-is-half-full" kind of person, do you get bombarded with negative thoughts?

I used to obsess over a part of my life which was veering off course and I would try to convince myself that if I could just solve that *one thing*, happiness would be around the corner. My mentality was like watching an infomercial. If you actually sit and watch more than a few minutes (yes, I am speaking from experience), you can be convinced that your life would be complete *only if* you could cut your hair with your tank vacuum cleaner... or *only if* your blanket had built-in sleeves... or if you *could just have* a sleek turban instead of a bulky towel to dry your hair.... Similarly, I used to focus solely on one area of my life at a time. I'd either give my attention to my heart, my mind or my body. It was an "either/or" kind of approach.

Then I experienced the most incredible blessing. I went into heart failure when I was 28 years old. Does that sound crazy? Well, stay with me for a second. When I flat-lined on the operating table and had out-of-body experiences, I quickly realized how every part of our being works together. It is vital to have a healthy heart *and* mind *and* body. It gave me a whole new perspective of the Apostle John's words to his dear friend

Transformation by Truth

Gaius, *"Beloved, I pray that you may prosper in all things and be in health, just as your soul prospers." (3 John 1:2 NKJ)*

If you've been approaching your life in bits and pieces, I pray that your eyes will be opened to the truth... the glory of your whole self. I pray that you may prosper in all things... that your body will be healthy... that your heart and mind will not be merely surviving, but thriving. Have you ever thought, "Yeah, that's great for everyone else, but this doesn't apply to me"? Well, do I have news for you! Here's what God says, *"For I know the plans I have for you," declares the LORD, "plans to prosper you and not to harm you, plans to give you hope and a future." (Jeremiah 29:11)* Why would God want to prosper *you*? Why does He want to give *you* hope and a future? Because He loves *you* beyond measure!

And I pray that you, being rooted and established in love, may have power, together with all the saints, to grasp how wide and long and high and deep is the love of Christ, and to know this love that surpasses knowledge—that you may be filled to the measure of all the fullness of God.

Now to him who is able to do immeasurably more than all we ask or imagine, according to his power that is at work within us, to him be glory in the church and in Christ Jesus throughout all generations, for ever and ever! (Ephesians 3:17-21)

God is able to do immeasurably more than what you can ask or imagine! This applies to your heart *and* your mind *and* your body.

In my hometown, I coach a fitness boot camp. The sessions last for four weeks since most experts agree that it takes somewhere between 21 and 30 days to create new habits. It's not your typical extreme workout where you sweat, shake with

Introduction

fatigue, pray that it ends, and then go home. Each weekday morning our team works out together, but instead of focusing exclusively on our physical fitness, we chisel our hearts and minds along with our bodies. This unique format is highly successful... so successful that I wanted to share it with others outside of our neighborhood.

This 30-day program will take you through similar life coaching steps in the form of heart, mind and body "applications." If you apply these concepts to your day-to-day living, you'll become a triple threat. You'll have a healthy heart, mind and body. To get the most of these 30 days, I recommend you journal your thoughts. It makes no difference if it's the fancy leather kind or a spiral-bound pad that you bought at the dollar store. As you write, your revelations will not only be engraved on paper, but also in your mind and heart.

Are you ready to be filled to the measure of *all* the fullness of God? Awesome. Let's get this 30-day party started....

Day 1

When I travel for work, I pack the lightest clothes I have because a third of my suitcase is allocated specifically for food. Am I a picky eater? Well, chances are decent I'm not the kind of picky that you might think. I enjoy every ethnic food, most meats, cheeses, fruits and vegetables. Basically, I love food. My mind gets obsessed on planning my next meal. However, I won't consume caloric food if it's not decadently worth every bite. That's where my pickiness comes into play. So, I fill my suitcase with turkey jerky, almonds, instant oatmeal, packs of tuna... basically, whatever you find at a health food store that's shelf-stable is probably in my luggage. That way, when lunch rolls around and I'm in the middle of a huge herd lining up at a buffet line, I don't have to eat the saucy egg foo yung. On a side note, that egg foo yung was inevitably made from the same shrimp that was served at the previous night's dinner in the form of shrimp cocktail, but who's keeping track, right? Packing my secret stash of healthy food also means I won't pop the button on my cute black pants.

This strategy mixed with my non-negotiable workouts really pays off. But there was one time when something went awry. I was at a company meeting with about 300 other people. The entire day I carried my backpack which held all of my documents, a journal for note taking, my Blackberry and most importantly my food. My healthy alternatives were awesome for breakfast and lunch. But after dinner, we had a special event planned. Gossip broke out and I found out we were being treated to a concert after we ate. Knowing that, the last thing I wanted was to be carrying a food-filled purse

Transformation by Truth

because everyone knows dancing and purse-holding don't mix. I ended up ditching the lean food I packed that night. I figured I could make a salad, find some chicken to put on top, and my waistline and I would be safe.

Think again. There was a meat carving station that had some sort of fatty red meat. My friends tried to tell me, "Marbling is just another word for flavor." I'm not sure. That big hunk o' fatty meat (oops... I mean *flavored*) just wasn't something I could stomach. Too bad really, because that was the healthiest thing out there. So, I ate a dinner roll knowing I'd eat after the concert when I got back in my room. It wouldn't have been a big issue if it weren't for the fact that I'm highly prone to low blood sugar if I don't eat well-balanced meals in regular intervals.

As I walked from the food troughs down the hallway to the ballroom, I felt like the room was slowly caving in on me. Tiny beads of sweat were forming on my face and on the top of my head. I knew where this was heading and it wasn't good. I dread hypoglycemic moments: my heart races, I feel incredibly weak, I can't stop sweating and I desperately need sugar. Embarrassed, I told my friends I had to go to the bathroom. Along the way, I cut in front of a line at a bar and asked for two glasses of cranberry juice. I guzzled those down and headed for a bathroom stall to lock myself in. Praying that no one recognized my shoes, I sat on the toilet and dabbed my sweat off with toilet paper for a good ten minutes. Finally the sugar from the cranberry juice calmed my body down and I was ready to go find my friends.

I was nervous to look in the mirror because I figured my makeup would have been blotted off from the toilet paper and my hair is notorious for getting really big and frizzy when it meets with humidity or any kind of moisture. So I decided to

Day 1

walk out without taking a glance at myself. As I had my hand on the door, I had a second thought. I'm pretty sure it was God's prompting because you should have seen my reflection. Actually, I'm so glad you didn't. Did you grow up with your parents harping, "Don't put anything in the toilet besides toilet paper!"? Do you know why that was so important? Because toilet paper, unlike Kleenex, disintegrates... it easily breaks down and does no harm to your home's plumbing. How does that translate to my situation? It disintegrated easily from my sweat. I had about fifteen little balls of toilet paper covering my face! No, I didn't want to look in the mirror because I feared the truth. But thank God (literally) that I did so I could fix the truth and create a new one.

APPLICATIONS

Heart:

> *Into your hands I commit my spirit;*
> *redeem me, O LORD, the God of truth. (Psalm 31:5)*

> *Surely you desire truth in the inner parts;*
> *you teach me wisdom in the inmost place.*
> *Cleanse me with hyssop, and I will be clean;*
> *wash me, and I will be whiter than snow. (Psalm 51:6-7)*

It's not necessarily fun to face the truth... especially when we know we are being called to a higher standard... a bigger life. Fun or not, it's necessary. Facing the truth gives us a basis for improvement. I'm not a typical female. I loathe shopping. So, when I go to the mall, the first thing I look for is the directory that has a red dot which says, "You are here." Once I find that dot, I can figure out how to navigate

Transformation by Truth

my way to the one and only store I want to go to, and then I can quickly go back home. What does your heart's "You are here" red dot say? What is the truth in your heart? Having a truthful foundation, you'll have a map to guide you where you want to go.

I want to share a few red dots I've had over the past handful of years. For the longest time, I neglected my heart. I went to church because it was the "right" thing to do. I brought two Jolly Ranchers candies and knew by the end of the second one, it would be time to hear the pastor's closing prayer and I was outta there. I checked off the God-thing on my list of things to do and moved on. Eventually I became more serious and created a new "You are here" dot. I would actually listen to sermons and try to apply the lessons to my everyday life. Now my red dot is in a place where I seek God everyday on my own accord, yearning for a deep, intimate relationship... but I can be honest and say that at times I can still catch myself barely getting through a hectic day and I realize I didn't live it *with* Him.

Where is your relationship with God right now? Where do you want it to be? Find your red dot and find your destination. Most importantly, open yourself up to giving God all of you. He desires you to be truthful with every ounce of your being... even in the ugly areas you'd never want to admit to a single soul. He loves everything about you! All the toilet paper balls on your face are not a surprise to Him, nor do they make Him love you less. Right where you are is a perfect starting point! In your journal, write a letter to God explaining where your red dot is now, including all of your toilet paper balls and ask Him to wash you white as snow as you open yourself up to an intimate relationship with Him.

Day 1

Mind:

What about the state of your mind? Do you even give thought to your mental health? If so, write about your red dot in your journal. Where are you now? Where do you want to go? What are your toilet paper balls? If you're not sure, take a notepad or your journal with you today. Each time you are aware of your thought process, write it down. For instance, on your drive to work, are you already upset with your co-workers and your boss before you take your first step into the office? Have you ever found yourself replaying a fight you had with your spouse like it was a broken record in your mind (yes, I am still stuck in 1970's technology)? Or maybe you're someone who is faced with a possible layoff at work and the voices in your head tell you that you're not valuable enough to find a new job.

Another way to get an objective viewpoint on your mental health is to focus on the words that come out of your mouth for a day. Five years ago, I was driving with my four-year-old daughter and we were running late to an appointment. I had to stop for a pedestrian who was crossing the street. My daughter sarcastically said, "Oh, come on lady!" Ugh. She was like a parrot, so I quickly knew that I needed to focus on the words I spoke. Catch yourself today and pay close attention to what comes out of your mouth. How do you respond when someone offers you a compliment? Are you able to graciously say, "Thank you"? Or, do you quickly explain that you really aren't worthy of the remark and turn your attention to them? Do you talk about others when they are not there? Are your words more "colorful" than what they should be? Are you self-deprecating? Do you complain often? This is a very telling way to know what is happening in your noggin.

Transformation by Truth

Whatever is on your mind, write it down and summarize those thoughts in your journal. Describe where you are today and where you'd like to be.

Body:

How do you judge your physical fitness? I typically go off of the numbers on the scale, my body fat percentage and my doctors' wisdom. That works for me. However, I find that many of my friends and clients, even many who are in perfectly great shape, fear stepping on a scale. When this is the case, I tell them to find other objective measurements. Here are a few ideas: use a measuring tape and record your body measurements; get a pair of jeans to measure how tight or loose they are; or step on a scale and let someone you trust such as a friend or a personal trainer (someone who encourages you, with no ounce of weird undercurrents) monitor the numbers for you. How are you defining your starting point? Write your objective foundational measurements and the changes you want for yourself in your journal.

Phewww! We have it all down on paper! So now here's where you start: take full responsibility for your truth-filled, current situation. The very moment it's not someone else's fault and the moment you decide that circumstances don't matter... you are in business! And here's what's exciting about your starting point: Jesus said in Matthew 9:13, "For I have not come to call the righteous, but sinners." He came for those of us who found toilet paper balls, not for those who were "perfect."

With God's help, you are going to create the most amazing you! Being truthful and creating a starting point for your spiritual life, your mental health and your physical fitness is a huge first step. In

Day 1

fact, the act of bringing all the toilet paper balls out of hiding and into the light will already begin your heart, mind and body improvements—pay close attention to the tiny steps you take today in the right direction and celebrate the beginning of this journey!

If you want to kick your plan up another notch today, <u>Appendix A</u> outlines how to start a workout plan.

Day 2

Have you ever had an event that rocked your world to the point where the date will be etched in your mind for a lifetime? Wednesday, July 7, 1999 started out with sheer excitement. I had a phone interview first thing in the morning for a promotion at work. Notice I used the words "excitement" and "interview" in the same breath. It's not that I had an overwhelming amount of self-confidence, but since upper management asked me to apply for the opening, I thought it would be a big day that would change my life. Wow, was I ever right....

I remember answering questions with ease, and I could literally feel my exaggerated facial expressions throughout my replies. And then, randomly, I felt this pressure in my chest. Lacking a better description or technical expertise, all I can say is I felt a "whoosh" along with the quick burst of heaviness in my chest. After that, I could hear my heart beating in my ears. I pressed the phone closer to the side of my head, struggling to hear the interviewer's voice on the other end. Thoughts ran through my mind, "Why am I panicking like this? Maybe I *am* anxious after all...."

Wednesdays were my Mom's cancer treatment days. Those were days when I got to my parents' house at 2:30 in the afternoon and drove my Mom to her doctor's office. My sister Lori met us at the infusion room and we both kept our Mom company while she got her chemo and then I would drive my Mom home. We would make dinner for our Dad while we got our Mom settled in bed. At that point, Lori would take over all of the nighttime responsibilities. But it was not a normal day.

Transformation by Truth

I was fatigued. There was a lethargy lingering that I hadn't felt before. My solution? Caffeine. When that didn't help, I added food. But nothing was cutting through the cloud around me. Once we arrived at the doctor's office, one of the nurses shared her concern about the blood banks being low. Well, my Mom often needed blood transfusions due to the progression of her cancer, so I decided to donate blood downstairs in the hospital. The phlebotomists knew me and my sister well and affectionately called me "Bubba" since I was the bigger (as in larger, heavier) sister who weighed enough to donate blood. Lori clocked in under 110 pounds even with her funky platform shoes. After the routine screening, they found no reason why big 118-pound Bubba couldn't donate blood that day. Poke!

But after that, things went south. I remember telling Lori I wasn't sure if I could get our Mom home. With all grace she replied, "Go home Noey. Get rest. I've got everything covered." Don't ask me how I drove home that evening because I don't remember. Hey! I have no affiliation with Dionne Warwick and her psychic network of friends (bad 80's infomercial)… but did you just have an Asian driving joke run through your mind? If so, I hope you feel guilty.

Anyway, by the time I got home, I was struggling to get enough air. It felt like I was breathing through a straw. Panicked, I called a couple of my physician friends and told them I had just donated blood and I was short of breath. I spared them the details of the rest of my day, which was to my detriment. So, they both responded by saying, "Drink water and get rest. You'll be fine tomorrow." I did as they said until each breath became so labored, it felt like I was underwater in a pool trying to breathe.

Day 2

I debated whether or not to call my Dad and ask for help. The last thing I wanted to do was place an extra burden on his shoulders. As it was, he was watching his bride of 38 years slowly lose her fight to stage four colon cancer. After that battle in my head, I called him at 8:00 p.m.

"Hello?"

"Hi Dad, it's Noelle. Are you busy?"

What I didn't know until months later was, yes he was busy. In fact, he was preparing a very important speech he had to give the next day to a large, influential audience. Had I known this, I never would have troubled my Dad with my problems.

"Why do you ask?"

"Dad, I might be the kid who cried wolf, but I feel really bad."

"I'm coming to get you right now. We're going to the emergency room."

APPLICATIONS

Heart:

Yet the LORD set his affection on your forefathers and loved them, and he chose you, their descendants, above all the nations, as it is today. (Deuteronomy 10:15)

It wasn't only when I was dealing with my Dad... but whenever I approach anyone, I typically take a defensive stance. If I see the tiniest sign that they might have other things on their minds, I apologize and dismiss what I was planning to share. The reason I do this is because I tend to struggle with my self-worth and I don't want to be a bother. In this situation when I approached my Dad, I could have looked at this from his perspective. He was my DAD! I was his little girl. His heart for me was beyond description. He loved me more than words could explain. Of course I wasn't bothering him. If anything, he would have been heartbroken had I not run to him, my Daddy, first.

This is a perfect illustration on how we approach our Heavenly Father. Have you ever withheld your burdens from God because you think He has bigger things to deal with? Take the time to comprehend that God intentionally chose *you... above all nations.* YOU! Grasp His immense love and affection. You are important, and you matter to Him! Resist the urge to compare your situation to someone else's. God cares deeply about you. He doesn't have anything more important to tend to above you. Understanding this is an essential foundation of your transformation.

In your quiet time, ask God why He chose you... ask Him what is so special about you. Take the time to be still and wait upon His answers. My husband taught me early in our relationship that God "speaks" by weighing feelings on our hearts, or putting thoughts in our minds. If we're not sure if those thoughts are from Him, we can search the Bible to see if the messages are consistent with God's character. Write these revelations in your journal.

Mind:

You can't live a perfect day without doing something for someone who will never be able to repay you. –John Wooden

Day 2

I think we can all agree that the most valuable gift we can give someone is the gift of our time. But in today's world, it's sadly becoming more elusive. How would you reply if someone asked you, "Are you busy?" on a day when your tasks were as steep as Mount Everest? Are you someone who, like my Dad, would question, "Why do you ask?" Or could you have possibly dismissed the opportunity at hand by saying, "Yes, I'm so busy. You have no idea how much I have on my plate right now!" This has certainly convicted me. It showed me just how much I have *me* on my mind!

The moment I get in front of my computer seems to be the exact time when my daughter needs to ask me a question. I've gotten to the point where I have started to pray when this happens because everything in me wants to tell her to go do something else. But I want to be the kind of person who follows in my Dad's footsteps and I want to realize that every time I give her my full attention, I'm giving her an invaluable gift which she will never have to pay back. I'm making deposits into her memory bank which are far more precious than any amount of money.

What can you do today to make sure that your mind is not consumed by yourself? Since you are taking actions on your heart, mind and body... and since you are taking these actions while believing that God loves you with abandon... you are now able to free up your mind. You know that you matter, and now you can let those around us know that they matter too. Consider your lonely neighbor, a grandparent, an outcast at work and of course your family and close friends. Journal the action you can take today to show one person that they matter. Do this out of pure generosity and release them from the obligation of ever having to repay you.

Transformation by Truth

Body:

Has your body given you any warning signs? They don't need to be as drastic as the warning signs I had that day. Are you lacking the energy you should have through your day? Is your weight making you physically uncomfortable? Maybe you're someone who would have more self-confidence with a stronger, leaner body. Whatever it is, commit to take action immediately. Add a minimum of 30 minutes (but an hour would be nice) of intentional physical activity into your calendar five days per week, including today. For at least two of those days, add in strength (weight) training as a non-breakable appointment. When you look at your calendar, certainly you can find 30 minutes of spare time… don't pretend that you can't. Check out <u>Appendix A</u> for ideas.

For me, I workout before my day begins. This way, I don't have to try and fit it into the middle of a chaotic day. My workouts also give my morning the energy boost that I need to conquer my day. There is convincing data which shows that people who exercise in the morning sleep better at night. I teach boot camp at 5:30 a.m. At the beginning of every four-week session, I typically have one or two people who swear they are not morning people. By the end of the four weeks, they usually convert. Here are some of their tips:

- Get to bed earlier! Even if you are not used to it, create a relaxing pre-bedtime routine and enjoy the luxury of rest.
- Sleep in your workout clothes. Crazy, I know—but it has worked for several boot campers. Others lay out their clothes the night before, right next to their bed.
- Set an alarm clock to give you a few minutes of non-hurried time to drink water (8-20 oz) and get something

Day 2

in your stomach such as a banana or blend up a quick smoothie that is carb-based. I also have a cup of coffee, but it's certainly not a necessity (although it is for *my* mood).

- Try a workout where you get used to seeing others for camaraderie and accountability such as a class at the gym or join a walking or running group.

If this doesn't work for you, take a good look at your schedule and find a pocket of 30 minutes to an hour where you can schedule your workouts in as a non-negotiable appointment with yourself!

Day 3

Once we arrived at the emergency room and I checked in at the front desk, I tried every chair and continuously repositioned my body looking for some level of comfort. I eventually ended up on the ground in a fetal position trying to regain my breath. My sister and her boyfriend heard the news and cut their date short in order to be with me and my Dad. My name was called and when I was taken to the back, I was firmly told, "I am only measuring your vitals, and then you will go back to the waiting room until we have room for you."

I stuck my arm out and the blood pressure machine buzzed. When it finished, without explaining her actions, the medical assistant left me alone and came back with a different machine. I stuck my arm out again and the machine buzzed just like the first one. She quickly left the room again. "Ugh… am I stuck in a time warp?" I thought. This happened for a third time. The third machine and the third time confirmed the original results. The first two machines were not broken as she thought. No, the numbers on all the machines read the same. My blood pressure was 60/18 and my pulse was 180. I didn't realize the significance of her findings, so I expected to go back out into the waiting room with my Dad and Lori.

You can imagine my confusion when they suddenly found a room for me and there was a tornado of chaos around my bed. One nurse told me she was placing a catheter in me. I pleaded with her, "Please don't! I'll be fine. Catheters are painful, right?" Of course I had no idea that I was in heart failure and the catheter was the least of my worries. "Can you please give me something to help me breathe?" There was no answer to my question. In fact, from that moment, I was given very little eye contact and it seemed as though everyone was avoiding conversation with me. An IV was started. I was being poked and prodded and I had no idea why.

An x-ray technician wheeled my bed downstairs for a series of radiology tests. Trying to maintain a speck of my personality, I asked him if this is what a girl needed to do to get a good looking guy to cater to her. He smiled but didn't reply. Immediately upon completion, I was back upstairs. A different nurse came in and said, "This should help your breathing." A rubbery covering was put over my nose and mouth. I was so excited for the idea of taking a deep breath of fresh air. The mist added moisture and I breathed in deeply to no avail. It felt the same. In fact, the deeper I breathed, the more I choked. The mask was removed. Another nurse came in with a different one, "Try this." Again I took a deep breath. It felt like water went down the wrong pipe and I couldn't stop coughing and choking. Every time someone ran by my bed, I would hesitantly ask, "Excuse me. Am I okay?" There wasn't a single person who answered my question. There have been times in my life when I have felt like an outcast, but nothing to this degree.

A sight for sore eyes! In addition to the attending emergency room physician, my nephrologist, Dr. Ahdoot was called in for my case. You have no idea how much I love this man. I expected to tell him how I felt, and then as always, he'd have a solution to relieve my pain. But, instead I only glanced at him from a distance. He was talking non-stop on the phone. His voice was strong but hurried. A nurse came by and asked, "Honey, do you want me to bring your Dad in?"

"Actually, the only person I want is my sister." All of my hope had faded and the deepest part of my spirit cried out to God. My sister was the only person in my immediate family who embodied Jesus in her heart. Above any motivational talk, more important than any amount of positive thinking, is the search for God's intimacy and His truest presence. Lori was brought to my side. There wasn't a lot of conversation, but from her heart she exudes compassion that is indescribable—you can see it in her eyes. She asked how I was and tenderly inquired if I had any fear. She then gave me the only gift that could calm my soul: she lifted me to God and prayed over me. When she finished, she spoke the words I had hoped to hear all night, "You're going to be okay." I realized at that moment, the words were from God. I wasn't sure if I was going to be healed on a physical level, but I knew He was letting me know that I was going to be okay from an eternal perspective.

APPLICATIONS

Heart:

I had never hit rock bottom like this before. I typically can see the silver lining in the clouds, but in that moment, all I could see was the storm. Have you ever hit rock bottom in your life? Have you been faced with a diagnosis that has stolen your hope? Maybe you've lost a loved one and the devastation is overwhelming. Is your marriage going downhill fast despite your most valiant efforts? Has your weight increased dramatically? Have diets failed you? Are you finding how unbelievably difficult it is to overcome addiction?

In my case, I put all my hope into the nurses and then the doctors. I couldn't believe that at 28 years old, they didn't have a textbook solution for me. Throughout my day, up until the moment Lori was brought to my bedside, I was looking to everything and everyone to help me. Everyone except the one true Healer. Have you sought healing from sources that have left you unfulfilled?

But seek first his kingdom and his righteousness, and all these things will be given to you as well. (Matthew 6:33)

Rock bottom times are typically in our lives because we've been dealt devastating blows which have broken our hearts. I can't begin to tell you how much of my life I have had this instruction from Matthew 6:33 backwards. In fact, I still catch myself in wrong thought patterns. Instead of seeking God and His righteousness first, I would give Him a wish list of things *I* thought would patch my brokenness back together. But if we simply look to our Heavenly Father, what do we find out about His character? All of these verses have a common theme—God's deep longing to heal our broken hearts: Psalm 23:1-3; Psalm 147:3; Malachi 4:2; Matthew 13:15; Luke 9:11. He won't force Himself on you, but He would love for you to invite Him into the deepest desires of your soul (Revelation 3:20).

Read Psalm 23. Find your own "quiet waters" by turning off all technological gizmos and finding a place of solitude. Respond to Revelation 3:20 by inviting your Heavenly Father to speak to your heart, heal your brokenness and restore you so you can live on a whole new level. During your prayer time, use your faith by knowing that Jesus is right next to you. Give Him total access to your heart—including every detail that you try to hide from the world: all of your embarrassment, all of your disappointments, all

Day 3

of your fears and all of your faults. He will listen to you with incomparable compassion and perfect understanding. He will hold you through your agony and draw you into Himself. Ask for God's guidance so you can discern what He reveals to you. James 1:5 tells us that God generously gives wisdom to us when we ask. What are you discovering by God's revelation?

Don't try to hurry this critical process. This may take many restoring conversations. Let God uncover the lies that you have been living by. Inquire about forgiveness. Maybe you need to repent and ask for forgiveness for your faulty ways of dealing with your brokenness or you might need to let go and forgive those who have deeply hurt you. Let Him show you where Satan has created strongholds in your heart and find out what the truth really is. Finally, ask for Jesus to take all of those jagged pieces and restore your heart to be wonderfully whole.

His truth will heal you and allow you to feel freedom regardless of your current circumstances, giving you the power to dream big dreams and face your day with unmatched encouragement (John 8:32). Journal the steps you feel led to take whether it's looking for a counselor, reading a book that can bring deep healing for your wounds, or just maintaining the habit of having daily quiet times. Make sure your calendar reflects your action steps!

Mind:

Instead of seeking God's hand for what He can give you, focus solely on seeking His face through faith, imagination and visualization today. Find a scripture which promises hope for your deepest wound by using a concordance to search by subject or keywords. If you don't have one in the back of your Bible or if you don't have a Bible, you can use an online resource such as www.biblegateway.com and search by topic or keyword. Write your verse(s) on an index card and keep it with you all day. If you can't find one, Jeremiah 17:7 might speak to your heart, *"But blessed is the man who trusts in the LORD, whose confidence is in him."* Repeat it until you know it by memory. Keep the card somewhere where you will see it often.

Body:

Yesterday you put your workouts in your calendar and you started moving, right? If not, get moving immediately! We all reach a point in time when we really mean business when it comes to changing our bodies. For many of us, it's when we hit some sort of a rock bottom and we are so unhappy with ourselves that we must make a change. List all of the pain, both literally and figuratively, associated with your current body. Use this list to remind you throughout these 30 days why this pain is worse than the temporary discomfort of exercising and eating well. Don't worry… any pain you have now will subside as you create new habits and evolve into an athlete.

You know you need the change. In addition to your scheduled workout (not instead of, but in addition to), make a commitment to add things into your life today. We are not talking about deprivation! Add more movement by taking the stairs, park further away from your destination, dance and be silly at home whether or not someone is watching. Add more pure, fresh water and produce to your nutritional plan. In your journal, list all the activity that you are committing

Day 3

to add to your day in addition to your scheduled workouts. Then list what you are going to add to your day nutritionally. Let's lift you out of your rock bottom, and head toward making your bottom a rock! (Come on... a little fitness humor never hurt anyone!)

Day 4

I remember back when my Mom got diagnosed with terminal cancer and was in the midst of surgeries and chemotherapy. She lost her hair. She was nauseous and vomited the majority of her days. Since we rarely had heartfelt conversations, it felt awkward and embarrassing as I sobbed, "Mom, I am so sorry for all that you are facing. I wish I could take your place." Her eyes welled up with tears as she replied, "I feel worse for you since it's harder to be the caretaker." I never believed her words until the roles were reversed and my sister became my caretaker.

Lori put extreme thought into each of her actions. Just recently she explained that there was nothing she wanted more than to be at my bedside, but she also wanted to hear Dr. Ahdoot on the phone. As my big sister, she sought educated wisdom in case she had to make critical decisions on my behalf. So she kept one ear attentive to me and the other listened to every detail my doctor spoke. Lori expressed immense gratitude for Dr. Ahdoot. The night I had heart failure, he was very intent on the phone, coordinating the most highly-esteemed medical staff to care for me. He immediately called Dr. Alimadadian, the best cardiologist for my case and Dr. Ott, a premier thoracic surgeon. Dr. Ahdoot's dedication to me makes my soul ache with appreciation and love.

After Lori prayed over me, I had to remove the mask on my face because with each inhalation came a stark rattling sound; and as I exhaled, I began choking and vomiting. Remembering back, Lori said she was remarkably stunned that I was so calm when I began throwing up pink fluid. My fear must have come across as quiet composure. In hindsight, I realize that was a measure God used to protect my sister's heart because internally I was anything but calm. Once the medical staff saw the pink fluid, the chaos around me increased in log rank form (this math analogy should impress my friends since I defy the odds by being a Japanese girl who lacks the math gene). But Lori and I didn't know the implications of what was happening.

The significance, it turned out, was frightening. The mitral valve in my heart had ruptured earlier in the morning, so although my heart was pumping as fast as it could, the blood was pooling in my chest instead of going through my body. I was drowning in my own fluids. Dr. Alimadadian compassionately informed Lori that I had 15 minutes to live. The medical team debated whether they should sedate me and let me die peacefully, or if they should send me to a different hospital for emergency open-heart surgery. But, he gave the disclaimer that there were no guarantees.

He further explained that this would be an emergency surgery and there was no time to waste. Lori said after hearing those words, she became extremely scared. She realized how pressed for time they were and it seemed as though they weren't moving fast enough. And to add to Lori's dismay, they chose to sedate me. She assumed that meant imminent death. But as it turned out, they intubated to buy me some time, assembled a surgical team, and took the tubes out when the ambulance was set to transport me.

My cardiologist Dr. Alimadadian has a heart much like Dr. Ahdoot's. They live by a standard of professional excellence combined with deep compassion for their patients. Dr. Alimadadian didn't entrust my fragile body to the paramedics,

Day 4

so he personally rode with me and squeezed the bag which gave my body air for the entire 25-minute transport. Lori followed the ambulance in her own car, not knowing the status of her little sister's lifeless body. I understand that the paramedics had to drive Dr. Alimadadian back to the emergency room where his car was after he left me with the surgical team in the middle of the night. His office manager told me months later that he showed up to work on time just a few hours later and was the same amazing man as always.

Meanwhile, my Dad had left the hospital to wake my Mom up, even though it was the middle of the night after a day of chemotherapy. The four full days after her chemo treatments were notoriously horrible for her tiny body. Can you imagine waking up in your own physical torment only to find out that your daughter is in very critical condition? I literally cannot put myself in that situation. However, Lori explains that when my Mom entered the waiting room at the hospital, she was strong, yet soft and brilliantly loving toward me. She shined. Lori said the room didn't feel empty anymore, and it felt like the richest love in world.

APPLICATIONS

Heart:

"Even to your old age and gray hairs I am he, I am he who will sustain you. I have made you and I will carry you; I will sustain you and I will rescue you." (Isaiah 46:4)

I completely agree with my Mom's words after having had this experience. It was incredibly exhausting and overwhelming to be her caretaker, and I could see the same exhaustion on

Transformation by Truth

Lori's face as she cared for me. Have you ever found yourself beyond your limits because you are caring for others? Do you feel the weight of raising children? Caring for parents? Supporting your spouse? Are waves crashing on you when you consider the responsibility of work, friends, family or serving your church?

What would happen if you let God be your caretaker? How does the landscape of your challenges change when you read Isaiah 46:4? God promises that He will sustain you. He will rescue you. Is His promise time bound? In other words, do you think it only applies to people in biblical times? Does He change through the years (James 1:17)? If you are overwhelmed right now, ask God in your prayer time what He's calling you to.

When I was my Mom's caretaker along with my sister, God called me to rest. He gave me a network of friends who offered their help. So when I sought His ways to sustain and rescue me, I was called to say "Yes" when offers for help came my way. Wow, was that ever hard! I had to drop my pride and admit that even though I'd like the world to think I'm Superwoman, I'm just a girl! God also called me to laughter. In the midst of sorrow, He gave me date nights with Ryan that were heartfelt and hysterical. I learned that it was not only okay to have joy in the middle of hardship; it was a necessity for me. Journal what God impresses on your heart. It helped me to remember that God sometimes chooses to work through His people. How will you respond to His offers of sustenance and rescuing? Journal what you learn.

Mind:

I am careful not to confuse excellence with perfection. Excellence, I can reach for; perfection is God's business. —Michael J. Fox

Day 4

When I think of pictures of excellence, I think of my amazing doctors. Dr. Ahdoot will always be a monumental person in my life. His pursuit for my healing continued even after I was transported to the other hospital. It turned out that he didn't sleep a wink that night due to his concern for me. Instead, he scoured medical journals until 4:00 a.m. hoping to find something that might help me.

Dr. Ahdoot just recently told me how proud he was to be affiliated with Dr. Alimadadian. Dr. Ahdoot said that it's nearly impossible to get a cardiologist into the emergency room so late at night. But, when he explained his urgent need of a cardiologist for my case, Dr. Alimadadian said, "Yes, I'll be there right away." There was no wavering, nor was there any consideration of him handing me over to the paramedics for my transport. He set aside his physical exhaustion in exchange for the hope of saving my life.

On my first post-operative appointment with my surgeon Dr. Ott, I profusely thanked him, "You had to operate in the middle of the night, you had no sleep and you were completely at the top of your game. You saved my life." His reply? "I was just doing my job."

All of us have the call to be excellent. We don't have to be saving someone's life to be significant and to pursue excellence. Lucano is one of the groundskeepers at the Montage in Laguna Beach. Our family would never be able to afford a room at that unbelievably beautiful resort, but I do have my quiet times sitting on their benches overlooking the beach on the weekends. Lucano works diligently to keep the property immaculate. And, when he sees me walking up to my favorite bench, he greets me with his dashing smile and quickly rakes the already smooth ground and inspects it for any minute piece of trash. His excellence may not be noticed by many, but it makes my world.

How can you reach for excellence today? How can you distinguish it from perfection? Does it change your outlook when you realize that God recognizes your efforts whether or not people do (Romans 2:29)?

Body:

I have always struggled to achieve excellence. One thing that cycling has taught me is that if you can achieve something without a struggle it's not going to be satisfying. –Greg Lemond

Does that word "struggle" ring true to your fitness pursuits right now? A life coach I once had used to say, "The greatest hero is the one who slays the biggest dragon." List in your journal what your "dragons" are in regards to your workouts and your nutrition. Once you've listed your biggest struggles, write out how you will emotionally feel once you've slayed each of them. Take the time to really internalize the deep satisfaction you will gain by achieving this excellence.

What is one step you can take today with each of your dragons? If you aren't sure, take time to ask God for direction. Remember that He is your caretaker and He will sustain and rescue you. Is He offering sustenance through His people? Are there programs He's provided to rescue you? His offers are unique for each of us, so take the time to hear His plan for you. Once you do, strive not for perfection but for excellence. Go and get your body moving and fuel it well!

Day 5

Do you know that feeling of being rudely awakened from your sleep? To this day, my sister and I still laugh at how my Mom went about waking us up in the morning for school. There was never the welcoming tone of voice whispering, "Good morning sunshine!" in our rooms. No, she seemed to lean toward waking us up military-style, although I have no idea what it would be like to be in the military. She would open our doors, flip on the blinding light and yell, "Get up!" We would be in a fog as we'd try to get our eyes to focus.

That's not far off from how I felt as I was being wheeled into the operating room. I was somewhere between a dream and a far-fetched reality. There was chaos around my bed as I was being rushed through the corridors into the surgical area. I didn't know this at the time, but Lori was running alongside the medical team in shock. She silently watched as they squeezed a ball to give me life-sustaining oxygen.

I don't remember having her at my side, but I do remember the moment I arrived in the operating room. There were stark bright lights. The room was cold and sterile. I closed my eyes and I felt a cold, sharp sensation that traveled from the middle of my upper chest down a handful of inches. When I explained this to my surgeon months later, he said it made sense that I felt the incision run down my chest for my open-heart surgery because I was so close to dying; there was very little anesthesia they could use.

During my last coherent hours leading up to the emergency surgery, everything about my existence was frightening, painful and intolerable. I was either too hot or too cold.

I desperately wanted to breathe, but found myself drowning in my own fluids instead. So it was a welcome relief when my chest was opened and I was being operated on.

I found myself peacefully floating over my own body. It was as if I were lying on a glass floor facing downward, watching a movie. I could see the operation below. Within a blink of an eye, I was out of that scene and placed in an all-consuming light. The best word to describe that light is "indescribable." (I'll bet that makes perfect sense to all the other females, right?) Pure warmth penetrated all of my being. My first prominent thought was, "Ahh! I can breathe!" It felt wonderful. I was no longer too hot or too cold. I was perfectly comfortable. After so many hours of tension, this was the ultimate release. Just then, I was floating over my body again. I watched for only a few seconds, before I was back in the light. Interestingly, I was told months later that I had flat-lined twice on the operating table which coincides with these experiences.

And then it was like listening to an old record that abruptly scratched and screeched to a halt. Thoughts raced through my mind as if I were speaking them out loud, "Wait a second. Did I just die? That was it? Case closed? Twenty-eight years. Never been married, no kids. My parents will be devastated. How could they lose their younger daughter while being in the midst of their own battles for life? What will my sister do when all of us are gone?" I started to pray, "God, I am so confused. Am I supposed to follow you? Please tell me what to do." Before I could hear His answer, I was transported into a completely different world.

I heard a beep. I felt my chest rise. Another beep. My chest expanded again. The only problem: I wasn't breathing! Within a moment, I realized I was on life support. I couldn't

Day 5

open my eyes, I couldn't move my body and I felt like I had been run over by a truck.

For my family, the waiting room was immensely tension-filled. Dr. Ott came to tell them that he successfully implanted a mechanical mitral valve in my heart. Lori said she and my parents let out a big sigh of relief. But that respite was short-lived when he added, "I have to tell you, she is a very sick girl. Noelle is on life support; she is not out of the woods." Lori said they went from elation to pins and needles in a single breath.

APPLICATIONS

Heart:

If you were put in my situation and you found that your life had come to an end, would you have had any regrets like I did? Pretend you found yourself in God's magnificent presence. What would that moment look like? How would it feel? Is your relationship with God authentic, deep and loving where you would melt into His presence and weep with joy and longing for Him? Or would you feel insanely anxious—like you were on a first date, not really knowing who He is?

Think back to your first dating relationship. On your first date, you were probably as nervous as nervous gets. But your desire for that person was so strong, you wanted nothing more than to move beyond the uneasy first date jitters into a genuine relationship. You probably talked endlessly with your precious love. When we have that type of conversation with God, it is praying. Don't be intimidated. God is looking for a true relationship. He isn't impressed by the overly "religious." Look at how Jesus explains that principle in the parable of the Pharisee and the tax collector in Luke 18:9-14:

To some who were confident of their own righteousness and looked down on everybody else, Jesus told this parable: "Two men went up to the temple to pray, one a Pharisee and the other a tax collector. The Pharisee stood up and prayed about himself: 'God, I thank you that I am not like other men—robbers, evildoers, adulterers—or even like this tax collector. I fast twice a week and give a tenth of all I get.'

"But the tax collector stood at a distance. He would not even look up to heaven, but beat his breast and said, 'God, have mercy on me, a sinner.'

"I tell you that this man, rather than the other, went home justified before God. For everyone who exalts himself will be humbled, and he who humbles himself will be exalted."

Simply give God your heart by dedicating time to just be in His presence. Spending time together and communicating are the foundational steps of any relationship including one with God. What other things have you done to build relationships? Chances are you wrote love letters which lit your heart on fire. You can write those to God in your journal. You used your resources whether it was asking questions, or doing your detective work to know everything you could about your special someone's character. You can learn all about God's personality and character through the Bible, books and through great teachers.

We all have different ways to get close to God because we are all created uniquely. For Ryan, he savors his time with God in the midst of the beautiful mountains on a dirt bike or he'll take walks on hiking trails near our house and have silent conversations with God there. I cherish my quiet

$\mathcal{D}ay\,5$

times writing love letters to God while I'm sitting on a bench overlooking the beach. What are ideas you have that match your personality? Journal your responses. Which action are you taking today to deepen your relationship with God?

Mind:

That the birds of worry and care fly over your head, this you cannot change, but that they build nests in your hair, this you can prevent.
—Chinese Proverb

This saying cracked me up! Isn't it a great visual? Think about how many times you have let birds of worry and care "build nests in your hair." How many of those nests will actually matter when we reach the end of our story here on earth? But most of us are walking around with a lot of nests. What are your nests' names? A few of mine are: worry, perfection and bill-paying. I'll tell you what... none of those nests were on my mind and heart when I was on life support! So, how can you put your mind into the right perspective now?

Consider your nests. What type of advice would a wise, elderly person give you regarding each nest? Maybe it would sound something like this, "If I were to live my life over again, I wouldn't take things so seriously," or, "I'd take more barefoot walks in the grass, pick daisies and love with abandon." Can you imagine a pearl of wisdom that someone nearing the end of their time here on earth would share with you? What would their message be? Journal that advice. Implement that counsel this very moment. Today is a new, clean canvas to recreate your mind's perspective.

Body:

Have you ever thought that it shouldn't matter what you look like, it should only matter who you are inside? 1 Corinthians 6:19-20 says, *"Do you not know that your body is a temple of the Holy Spirit, who is in you, whom you have received from God? You are not your own; you were bought at a price. Therefore honor God with your body."* Look at the Holy Temple in the Old Testament. It was the figurative dwelling place of God's presence here on earth. But now He resides in the hearts of believers by His Holy Spirit. Whoa! Wait just a second. Do you get it? Do you see the connection?

Your body is where He lives! So, take a look... what instruction was given when the temple was broken down and needed repair? Carpenters, builders, masons and stonecutters were all called in to fix things (2 Kings 12:11-14; 2 Chronicles 24:12-14). Man, they brought in the big guns to honor God's dwelling place! Are you putting that same amount of attention to your body? Couple these ideas with the fact that you and I *"are God's workmanship, created in Christ Jesus to do good works, which God prepared in advance for us to do." (Ephesians 2:10)* That means that God can't do His work through you if your body can't take Him out and about. How much more effective would you be in blessing others if you had stronger endurance, more muscle strength and a healthy self-image?

Focus from this point moving forward on repairing and maintaining God's dwelling place. Start eating clean. This is a perfect complement to the workouts you started and the added movement you've committed to. I do an 80-20 split. I know, you're thinking, "Wait a second—this sounds like a sales seminar!" Eighty percent of my food is whole, unprocessed

Day 5

food, meaning it had a mother or it came from the ground, while 20 percent of it is whatever the heck I like assuming it is free from high fructose corn syrup (HFCS), trans fats (look for the key words "hydrogenated" or "partially hydrogenated" on the food label) and artificial sweeteners (saccharin, aspartame and sucralose). Yes I'll eat a chocolate sandwich cookie, but it might not be the brand name you'd recognize. I treat myself a little bit every single day, buying those splurges at a market that has healthier options, so I never feel deprived. See Appendix B for calorie guidance.

Journal everything you eat and drink and take notes on how you feel emotionally with each meal. While doing this, look for red flags. For instance, maybe you eat a lot of junk food at 5:00 p.m. everyday because you're famished. Try packing a snack to eat on your drive home from work such as an apple and a small handful of almonds so you never hit that ravenous hunger. Maybe you find yourself eating sweets after you put the kids to bed because you feel like you deserve a reward for making it through the day. How about a different kind of a treat such as a bubble bath with spa-like iced water with lemon slices? Fixes such as these are like putting a Band-Aid on a wound.

But, for wound prevention, we need to dig deeper. Pay close attention to the emotional notes you write in your food journal. Typical emotional reasons people overeat are: celebration (I got through the day… I deserve a treat), stress, depression, loneliness and boredom. When you see that your poor eating patterns correlate to unresolved emotions, you need to take action and *work* through them instead of *eating* through them! Read books to help you manage that particular emotion, use biblical references or seek counseling.

Don't expect perfection. We all slip up. When that happens, give yourself grace and then get back on track. View this process as exciting. You are uncovering a different, healthier person! It's time for you to think and act like an athlete!

Day 6

Shortly after we adopted Sierra and traveled back home from China, we had ten days of sleeplessness. I feel guilty even attempting to get compassion from parents of newborns, because I know that a mere ten days without rest for them would make them deliriously happy. But, as for me and Ryan, it only made us delirious. I knew my body was tipping over the edge when I went to the bathroom and after I finished, I realized I never took off my underwear. More information than you needed for sure, but I'm trying to make a point here. Got the picture? My apologies if you now have a visual that you just didn't need.

All that to illustrate that those post-adoption, exhausting days weren't even a blip on the Richter Scale compared to what I was experiencing on life support. The days were filled with taking one step forward, then two steps back. I was eventually able to open my eyes, but my lungs would fill up with fluid sending me into a deep panic. My doctors were thrilled when I seemed to be "getting out of the woods," only to have my lungs collapse and they quickly second-guessed their excitement. My breathing started to get stronger. So, without telling me what they were doing, technicians turned the knob down on my ventilator and I found myself unsuccessfully gasping for air.

Through all of the torment, God showed His immense care by blessing me with a living angel. My nurse Pam was about the same age as me. She had beautiful brown eyes, a tender smile and compassion so deep that it could only be from God Himself. When my lungs would fill with fluid

Transformation by Truth

(which was extremely often), I found a way to bang my arms against the side of my bed hoping that Pam would hear. Within seconds, her face would be inches away from mine. I can still hear her precious voice, "Okay sweetie, I am going to go from the top of my head to the bottom of my toes. When I speak what the problem is, blink your eyes for me." Almost immediately she would identify the excess fluid in my lungs.

Pam quickly got the tubing that would go down my throat to suction the fluid out. Even though it got to a point where this happened numerous times in a single day, she never neglected to tell me what she was doing each step of the process. "Here comes the tube. You are going to feel saline right now. Okay Noelle, I need you to cough up the fluid. You are going to be okay. I know it feels like you are choking. I got the fluid, so I need you to calm down and rest so the breathing machine can take over and breathe for you." She was my lifeline. I literally lived by each set of directions she gave me and I longed for her tenderness. I didn't grow up in a physically affectionate family, but I craved intimacy during those days. Pam innately talked to me with her face close to mine and she always held my hands.

My journey had come so far from the night in the emergency room, but I still hadn't heard the words I desperately longed for... to hear that I was going to be physically okay. I looked at Pam and used the best sign language I could muster as I pretended to write with a pen. "Do you want to write something to me? I'm going to trust that you won't pull out any of your tubes." My writing looked like a second grader's. The paper contained three words, "Am I okay?" Pam's eyes reflected her sympathy, "Oh sweetie, you work with me and I'll make sure you're okay." To this day, I can visualize the beauty of her eyes and I can hear her sweet voice.

Day 6

Months after my release from the hospital, I went back to the intensive care unit to thank her in person. Remembering the warmth of her embrace still brings me to tears. She hugged me and only let go of her grip long enough to hold my shoulders as she looked at my face to tell me how beautiful I was. I told her about all the fears I used to have and how it took every ounce of energy for me to bang my arms against the rails of my bed to get her attention. Her reply astonished me, "Noelle, I spent every minute in a chair right next to your bed. I was with you the whole time!"

Without a doubt, I know she was from God. Doesn't that sound just like Him? Can't you hear His voice telling you that you are beautiful? Can't you hear His words saying, "I have always been with you. I would never leave you!"

APPLICATIONS

Heart:

The Lord himself goes before you and will be with you; he will never leave you nor forsake you. Do not be afraid; do not be discouraged. (Deuteronomy 31:8)

Since I couldn't see Pam, I just assumed she was out and about, taking care of someone else. That parallels the way I used to view God. Who am I to ask for help with my insecurities and low self-esteem when there are children starving in this world? Well, God is 100 percent among those precious children and at the same time He is 100 percent with me. He is God! He would never... catch that word "never"... leave any one of us.

How would your life change if you really understood this? Can you comprehend that He's even closer than being in a chair next to your bed? What would happen if you lingered on every word He spoke... every direction... just like I did when Pam would take the fluid out of my lungs? Would that revolutionize your prayer life? Does it give you a different frame of reference when we are told to, *"...pray in the Spirit on all occasions with all kinds of prayers and requests." (Ephesians 6:18)*? What can you do today to rest in that abundant intimacy with the Lord? Journal your answer. Commit today to consult with God throughout your day, not just in your quiet time. Talk to Him in your mind and share your experiences with Him. If you need His direction, ask for it!

Mind:

Friends are angels who lift us to our feet when our wings have trouble remembering how to fly. —Anonymous

Pam was someone who brought her whole heart to her job. One question I wish I could ask her is, "Do you truly understand just how much your patients appreciate your tenderness and excellence?" It might be different if Pam worked on another floor of the hospital where patients could readily communicate with her. But Pam was in the intensive care unit. Most all of her patients were intubated and completely incapacitated. I would guess that nurses like Pam work tirelessly for patients whose lives are riding the border of death. They probably don't get much gratitude for their efforts. If anything, I would imagine they could be an emotional punching bag for the distressed family members.

Day 6

There were a couple of nights when I didn't have Pam as my nurse and those were some of the worst 12-hour increments I can think of in my entire life. Those nurses didn't talk to me, they got frustrated when they had to continually suction fluid out of my lungs and they weren't half as good as Pam on technical and professional levels. They did as little as possible. I found myself in the deepest panic when I didn't have Pam. Did she get thanked enough? No. Did she still bring everything she had? Yes. She is my angel here on earth.

Think of someone in your life who could use an angel here on earth. Make a call, write a letter or take time for a personal visit. Don't put it off! Let God work through you so this person can experience His intimacy and love.

Have you had any angels here on earth? If there is any way for you to reach them, what will you do to communicate your heartfelt gratitude? If there's no way to be in touch, how can you pay your thankfulness forward? Journal your answers and put them into action today.

Body:

When exhaustion hits, we need to be restored. No one should be at the breaking point of forgetting they still have underwear on! When you are dog-tired, what are your solutions? Let's take a look at a foundational issue: how many hours do you sleep at night? What's the quality of your sleep? Statistics may vary somewhat, but most show that about seven out of ten people experience frequent sleep problems.

Having a regular bedtime and wake-up time will help you set your body's natural clock. In order to get yourself ready for bed, how can you implement nighttime rituals? This doesn't have to be fancy or time-consuming, but how can you signal to your body that it's time to wind down? What would happen if you ixnay-ed television and late night eating and replaced those habits with positive, relaxing behaviors? Some examples might be: taking a warm bath, reading for a few minutes (I'm thinking a suspenseful book might not work!) or writing in a gratitude journal. Getting optimal sleep is not only beneficial for your mood, it actually improves your metabolism since important hormones, such as human growth hormone and leptin, which prompts your body to know when it's had enough food, are released when you sleep. Write down your plan for getting at least seven hours of good quality sleep each night.

Of course, I live in the real world just like you and I know that there are days when you're exhausted but you still have to be responsible. What do you do then? Do you reach for caffeine or sugary snacks? Are there certain times of the day when you hit these pitfalls? Instead of these artificial stimulants, which will take you further away from your ultimate transformation, aim for a 15-minute power nap. Oh, I know, I know. I can hear your voice in my head, "I don't have time for a nap!" Really? Well, since I can't debate you in person, at bare minimum, turn all the noise around you off and relax your muscles one by one. Journal at least one creative way to add rest in the middle of your day.

Another option, if you have some energy, is to get your heart rate up. Try taking a quick power walk even if it's within your office. One of my friends has an actual office with a door, so he keeps a jump rope on his doorknob. When he feels tired and wants to grab a snack, he does three minutes of jumping first and then reevaluates. Journal at least one way you can get your heart rate up in the middle of the day, in addition to your scheduled workouts, for a quick energy boost.

Day 6

If you're one who will be quick to reach for a caffeinated drink, reach for a bottle of water instead. Hydration is the best energizing drink. Instead of processed junk food, get some fresh fruit and a small serving of nuts. Clean up your desperate-for-energy-techniques starting now. How are you going to limit your caffeine to 200-300 milligrams per day and consume it no later than lunchtime? Keep in mind that a six-ounce cup of coffee has approximately 100 milligrams of caffeine; a six-ounce cup of tea has about 40 milligrams. That's six ounces. The large size drinks that come from your local barista can be around 16-20 ounces. Journal your ideas and responses.

What tactics will you commit to from here on when your exhaustion and temptations hit? At this point, you should have journal entries with ideas on getting enough sleep at night, adding rest in the middle of your day, and options which will keep you from overdosing on caffeine and sugary snacks. Keep on this wave of momentum. You'll feel such a sense of accomplishment and victory because you will have the deep knowledge that your healthy character is truly being formed!

Day 7

Doesn't it seem like the moment you get into an easy groove in life, a curveball is just around the corner? I grew accustomed to being on life support once my lungs stopped filling up with fluid. When my family and close friends came in to visit, I was able to squeeze their hands and open my eyes to acknowledge them.

I guess there was only one thing I had a hard time getting used to. Every waking moment, I obsessed over my intense thirst. Using my version of sign language, I would motion for a drink. Since my fluids needed to be significantly limited, I would either be given just a few ice chips or a sponge "lollipop" which contained less than an eye dropper full of water. This became so agonizing that I'd try to sleep my day away so I could get as far from my thirst as possible.

When I slept, I'd dream about drinking all different types of water. Sometimes I craved full pitchers with lemon slices in it, other times I would fantasize about diving into a pool of crystal clear drinking water. In every vision, I drank endlessly until my thirst was quenched… until… darn it… I woke up and my obsessive thirsty cycle would repeat itself again. This was the extent of my world day in and day out.

So, here's the curve ball: I was half-asleep and I heard my surgeon's voice say, "Take her tubes out." Another voice responded with hesitation. I don't remember what was said, but I knew there was grave concern that I wasn't strong enough to breathe on my own. "They need to come out now," he continued. Within minutes there was a medical team around me. My eyes were closed. I felt the long tube leave my lungs as it

Transformation by Truth

came out of my throat. I could feel the tension from the doctors and staff as they yelled back and forth while monitoring my situation. In panic, I put every ounce of energy I had into breathing.

To my glorious surprise, I seemed to be doing it... oxygen was put in my nose, but I was really doing it... I was breathing on my own! Someone hoisted me up and placed me in a wheelchair. They quickly wheeled me down the corridors into a regular hospital room! I was excited, exhausted, nauseous and light-headed. Sitting upright was extremely taxing on my body. The bright lights and nervous energy around me were too much to take in.

I remember closing my eyes as I was lifted and repositioned until I could feel that I was in a different bed. Then, I opened my eyes slowly, looked around and I saw my parents and Lori smiling victoriously. As if that wasn't enough to make me cry tears of joy, guess what was brought to me by a nurse? Juice! Water and juice were unlimited. Unbelievable. Jesus raised Lazarus from the dead, and He raised me to this awesome new life!

Although my body was incredibly weak, I'd stay awake as much as I could through the day to thoroughly enjoy all of the visits from my friends and family. I would fall asleep at night to the sweetest dreams. Just about every couple of hours, lab technicians would come in my room to take blood samples and read my vital signs. Each time they whispered how sorry they were to wake me up. "Are you kidding? Don't be sorry!" I replied. You see, every time I was woken up, it meant I was alive. What other patients viewed as a frustrating nuisance was an opportunity for me to meet a new soul—to hear about their lives, their families and their hopes and dreams. This

Day 7

was the perfect transition for me to enter into the gift of my God-given renewed life!

APPLICATIONS

Heart:

"(B)ut whoever drinks the water I give him will never thirst. Indeed, the water I give him will become in him a spring of water welling up to eternal life." (John 4:14)

Have you ever been thirsty, metaphorically speaking, but instead of a tall glass of pure water, you felt like you were given a couple of ice chips? I can guarantee you this: if you do not have a personal relationship with Jesus, you are living on ice chips, not living water! If this is speaking to you, please turn to Appendix C to learn what it means to be a Christian and to accept Jesus into your life.

Or maybe you know who He is, in fact, He's your Lord and Savior—but you keep Him at an arm's distance, afraid of the deep intimacy He would love to have with you. You've closed the doors on certain parts of your life, thinking you can do a better job managing those yourself. Welcome to my world—I've been there, done that... and I have to constantly check myself because these patterns so easily repeat. Well, guess what? That's living by sponge lollipops. Which areas of your life have you denied God access? For some, it might be their marriage... for others, it might be their finances... or maybe it's their addictions. Whatever they are, explain why you're afraid to relinquish control.

Look over your list of rooms where you are afraid to give the key to God. In faith, hear His voice gently telling you,

"I know the plans I have for you (insert your name here), plans to prosper you and not to harm you, plans to give you hope and a future."(Jeremiah 29:11)

Let's be real. You and I have white-knuckled those areas of our lives where we feared that God might answer our prayers in ways different than what we wanted. But how is your plan working for you? Is your solution prospering you? What do you need to do to hand over the keys to every area in your heart to our Lord? Journal your answers in the form of a prayer… a love letter to God!

Mind:

I've never appreciated life as much as I did the days after I got off life support. When the lab technicians came into my room, they walked in on their tip toes and it pained them to tell me that they were drawing my blood in the middle of the night. The reason being: they were used to being yelled at by annoyed patients who were upset that their sleep was being disturbed. For me, I enjoyed some of the richest conversations during those blood draws. The rest of the world was asleep, but I got to receive these secret gifts from God Himself.

How do you respond to unexpected conversations with people who are disrupting your to-do list? Are they nuisances or opportunities? List out all the people you will see today such as your family members, people you might see while you walk your dog, the barista at your coffee house, the cashier at the market, etc. What opportunities can you think of for each individual? It can be as simple as telling someone that their smile brightens your day. Implement those acts of kindness and notice how you not only change the world around you, but also how your world changes with this shift of perspective.

Day 7

Journal the difference you make by being generous with simple acts of kindness.

Body:

We're fools whether we dance or not, so we might as well dance.
—Japanese Proverb

Your life and body have been God-gifted to you. Have you taken this for granted? Most of us do. Imagine that you lost your ability to use your body. I mean really take a moment and vividly imagine what it would feel like. I was devastated (that's an understatement) when I couldn't move a single part of my body—including wiggling my toes or opening my eyes—throughout my first handful of days on life support. Is there anything you would have regretted not trying? Would there be something that you had tried before that you would want to do again if you regained the use of your body? Maybe it would be dancing, running a race for a specific cause, or riding tandem bikes with your family.

Now put yourself in my shoes when I was removed from life support and transitioned into a regular room—complete with unlimited water and the ability to talk and move again. What would it feel like if you were miraculously given a renewed life? What would you want to do with that gift of a newfound, functioning body?

Schedule your answer in your near future as a special event. Continue with your workouts so you are in prime condition for your goals. Don't forget to take pictures and journal your successes!

Also, continue to hydrate your body well. My experience illustrates just how vital pure, clean water is for optimal health. Nothing quenches your body's thirst like pure water. I used to be a diet soda addict. I probably have enough chemicals in my body from those years where I won't need to be embalmed when my body dies! But, since I broke those chains of addiction and replaced those chemical-laden drinks with pure water—my energy level has improved dramatically, my skin looks better and it even changed me emotionally.

You've probably heard many guidelines to judge how much water is sufficient. Some of the ones I've heard are: take your body weight divide it in half, and drink that number in ounces per day; others say drink eight cups (eight ounces each) per day; some say more, some say less. Whichever piece of advice you take, make sure your actions guarantee your success. I fill up my water bottles in the morning. I make sure I have 80 ounces with me, because that's how much my body thrives on. I know I hit my mark when all my water bottles are empty. What works for you? Journal and execute... Cheers!

End of Week One:

Celebrate Good Times, Come On!

Aside from getting me in the mood for more Kool and the Gang, that line also puts me in the mood to celebrate *you*! What do you think? Aren't there reasons for you to celebrate? You completed week one of your personal transformation. What? Did someone say, "I wasn't perfect?" Well good. It's nice to know that you are human. But you did find success, right? Of course you did. The mere fact you are putting yourself out there, taking on the challenge to shine brightly for God's sake... that is success!

So how are you going to celebrate? Let me give you a hint. If one of your goals is weight loss, it might not serve you well to celebrate by ordering a triple-scoop banana split. Nah, that would negate your workouts. Instead, keep your celebrations in line with your goals. Since you are aiming to be physically fit, why not give yourself the gift of a new fitness magazine? Or maybe you can afford a new workout t-shirt, a cool-looking water bottle or a healthy cookbook. If you have the budget, a massage would be heavenly.

What about your heart and your mind? How are you splurging there? Have you been eyeing a new journal at the bookstore? Maybe you don't have an extra dime to your name. Even that shouldn't keep you from having an amazing time through this process. One of my friends spoiled herself by having her husband watch their kids for an hour. She took a cup of coffee and enjoyed every sip as she had quiet time on a park bench.

Transformation by Truth

If you are reading this thinking, "That's nice for them, but I'm just going to keep on truckin' full speed ahead into my next week. I don't deserve to have fun in this process..." I'll tell you what... you sound like a stick in the mud! Join the party for heaven's sake. You weren't created to live a life of drudgery.

Break out the party hats and streamers... invite me over for the conga line! Woohoo!

Day 8

At the beginning of the holiday season, I turn into a peacock. I sway my tail feathers and strut with pride. Why? Every year before Thanksgiving Day, I have inevitably finished buying all of my Christmas presents. I don't mean to brag, but let me brag. By the time I shop for a turkey, not only is my gift list complete, but it is done within a very tight budget. I buy name brands on clearance at discount shops to get serious bargains. If there were medals given out for time-saving, cost-efficient and perfectly-thought-out gift giving, I'd be wearing the gold. Hmm, can you smell the foreshadowing of a huge fall?

Like an accomplished criminal, I make sure that my tracks are covered so there is no evidence of my thriftiness. That's why I only purchase clearance items if the bright-red price tag peels off without leaving a sticky residue. The item needs to be in impeccable shape and the box it's packaged in must be dent free. You get the picture. So, one year I strolled the gourmet food aisle at TJ Maxx. There were eclectic bottles of flavored oils, imported dried pasta and cappuccino mixes... but what really caught my eye was a beautifully unique container filled with chocolates.

Knowing one of my older aunts loves chocolate, I put it through my battery of tests: the price tag easily peeled up in one piece; the box was in perfect shape; and best of all, it was one penny shy of five dollars. Granted, this same aunt gave me a 100 dollar bill every Christmas. But I rationalized my cheap gift, thinking, "She certainly should understand that I'm in my first career out of college and she must know that I barely get by loading up on Taco Tuesdays at Taco Bell... and anyhow... given how the box looked... well... maybe I bought it from an art museum or something, right? RIGHT?!"

Christmas came and I graciously handed her the present. This petite Japanese lady is probably the same height as E.T. She is quiet and demure. As she accepted the gift, she smiled with her head tipped to the side. Just as I imagined, she looked at the gift and admired the beautiful box. She opened it and remarked how she just loved chocolate. It was all going as planned until... something went severely off track.

She decided to share her gift with the entire extended family. The next thing I knew, she was walking around passing out chocolates to all of my aunts, uncles, grandma, cousins... she didn't miss a single person. It wouldn't have been a bad thing if it weren't for the worst unexpected surprise. The chocolates were shaped like Cheetos and they must have been rather outdated because they had a crackled white coating. What came to my mind was petrified cat poop (not that I'm an expert on what that looks like, but I'm just sharing the facts). I remember looking at my sister with wide eyes mouthing the words, "Oh no. Look!" I'm not sure all of what she said back, but I do remember her saying, "Chocolates? From *where*?!"

Have you ever gone from brilliance to brainless in a blink of an eye? I felt like such a fraud. It was like the truth was uncovered and all of a sudden, I was naked and everyone saw the real me. Nakedness in the context of family is never a good thing.

Day 8

APPLICATIONS

Heart:

If you could have stepped into my mind at the moment when I saw the chocolates and my family members' reactions, you would have heard my own voice calling me an idiot.

Well, that parallels my life on a much bigger scale. I used to have horrible messages that plagued my mind all the time. They would sound something like this, "Oh yeah, you're really a Christian, eh? Do you really think God could love someone like you? Look at all your failures, all your lies. This world sees one side of you, but they don't see the *real* you. God knows the real you. You are a fraud!" Sadly, I bought into those lies... and they kept me from growing within God's amazing love. I mean my growth wasn't just stunted... it was completely stopped. Ugh. Was I going crazy? Or was there more than what met the eye?

The thief comes only to steal and kill and destroy; I have come that they may have life, and have it to the full. (John 10:10)

I love how John Eldredge explains this verse in *Waking the Dead*:

Have you ever wondered why Jesus married those two statements? Did you even know he spoke them at the same time? I mean, he says them in one breath. And he has his reasons. By all means, God intends life for you. But right now that life is opposed. It doesn't just roll in on a tray. There is a thief. He comes to steal and kill and destroy. In other words, yes, the offer is life, but you're going to have to fight for it because there's an Enemy in our life with a different agenda.

There is something set against us.

We are at war.

Ah ha! There is the source for those lies in your mind... and the source is not you and it is not God. So, now you are faced with this question: Are you going to agree with the enemy or side with God? This is a war after all. You are not a fraud. But if the enemy gets you to believe that you are, you will not be able to live the life that Jesus died to give you... you will be taken out of the battle. You need to suit up for this war. Read Ephesians 6:13-17 and put on your armor of God so you can stand against the enemy.

Are there any thoughts that have plagued you? What are the messages in your mind that contradict what God says about you? Do you feel worthless? Do you think that there is no hope for you when it comes to the trials you are facing? Make sure you catch this... this is a hugely important fact. The source of those lies is the enemy, who has many other names including the devil or Satan. How do you think Jesus would respond to each of your erroneous thoughts? Journal your answers.

Mind:

I have not failed seven hundred times. I have not failed once. I have succeeded in proving that those seven hundred ways will not work.

When I have eliminated the ways that will not work, I will find the way that will work. —Thomas Edison

If you are anything like me, you would agree that it is pretty easy to fall into the world of obsession when it comes to replaying failures in your mind. I wish I was exaggerating when I tell you that I didn't sleep for many, many days after that Christmas gift exchange. I would sadly lay in bed and flashes of the disfigured chocolates and every family member's facial expression replayed in my mind over and over again, like a bad movie rental.

But here's the moral of the story: without my many goof-ups, I wouldn't have such colorful stories to tell. And I have a strong suspicion that you have stories that would compete with mine. So what may have appeared to be a failure is actually an avenue for me to have something in common with others. That's not just true on a silly level, but it holds true on the significantly larger mistakes I have made in my life as well. I made some really bad choices as a teenager. Any one of those decisions could have resulted in dire circumstances. God doesn't waste a single one of our slip-ups. If there is someone who can relate to the angst of a teenager, it is me. I'm not trying to give wisdom from a lofty perch. I walked the exact same roads as many troubled teens. God can use me to heal others!

How can you reframe the past failures your mind obsesses over? How can God use you to impact others? Journal your thoughts. You have an opportunity to use your mistakes to further God's work instead of letting the enemy use your mind as his playground to destroy you. Whose team are you on?

Body:

Be who you are and say what you feel, because those who mind don't matter and those who matter don't mind. –Dr. Seuss

Have you ever stopped yourself from attempting to conquer a health-related goal because you are afraid to look like a fool? Do you get scared that if you miss the mark, others will think less of you? Here's the comedy: chances are they aren't even giving you any thought! Really. Think that through. Imagine someone next to you was courageous enough to try running. After two minutes, they were huffing and puffing so they slowed down and walked. Would you think less of them? Of course not! You either wouldn't have noticed because you had too many other things on your mind or you would have been impressed that they were starting on their road to victory.

What is the worst possible thing that can happen if you fell just short of your goal? You'd still be better off than where you are now, right? Get over yourself... lose the false pride and take some risks. The payoffs will be well worth it! So, write out your fitness and health goals disregarding any hint of fear that you might look like a fool. What do you really want? Write your answers in your journal. How will you implement your ideas today with your eating, hydration and exercise? Write them down and get moving!

Day 9

My first job out of college was selling copiers and faxes. If you've ever worked in an office building, you probably had a sign on your front door saying, "No Solicitors." That sign was to keep riff-raff like me away. I still shudder when I think back to the outfit I wore on my first day. Coming out of college, I didn't own a suit, nor did any of my friends. But guess who did? My Mom. She had an old-fashioned houndstooth blazer which she said would go perfectly with her cowl-neck sweater. If you can't quite picture it in your mind, think of an elderly 23 year old. I looked perfect if I were going to a social game of cribbage. What's cribbage? See, you just proved my point!

I was a wonderfully enthusiastic employee. I couldn't believe that this company was willing to pay me 19,000 dollars per year. "Hey Dad! If I get any commission, it'll just be gravy on top... I'm rich!" I'd go out visiting the small businesses in my territory. After knocking on door after door and hearing the same reply, "We'll call you if we need anything. We're fine right now," I would still go right back to the office and make my telemarketing calls.

When the receptionist answered, I'd ask for the CFO. When we role-played in training, the process seemed rather simple. Of course, I didn't even know what CFO's were or what they did. I guess it made no difference anyway because I never talked to a single one of them. "I'm sorry," the receptionists would answer. "He's not available. Would you like to leave a message?" In the beginning I wasn't even aware of how horrible my batting average was. But after getting hung up on time after time and being physically escorted out of every high-rise office building in the city, the failure started to take its toll.

Lucky for me, I became good friends with Shellee, a gorgeous Texan whose desk was right next to mine. Her friendship made the job tolerable. We found humor in just about everything. The laughter we shared brought needed rejuvenation. I can still hear her Texas twang asking me, "Where'd yew git thooose pantyhose? They don't even hug yer knees!" Shellee's husband dubbed us, "The Dynamic Duo." The good news was that we got a lot of attention from upper management including the VP and the CEO. The bad news was why they took notice of us.

After being knocked down enough, the job really wreaked havoc on my motivation and my self-esteem. So Shellee and I decided to go cold calling together. We visited the offices in her territory first, took a lunch break, and then we finished our day's calls in my territory. On our lunch break that day, we decided that instead of eating, we'd go to Nordstrom. It was a fantastic day until it ended with us, along with our manager, being called into the VP's office, "How was lunch today, girls?"

Feebly we answered, "Uh, fine?"

"How was Nordstrom? Our CEO saw you there."

Now, I still want to know what *he* was doing there... a mystery of the ages, I guess. Anyway, once we realized we weren't going to be fired, it has provided us decades of funny storytelling.

But there was one instance that brought us to a different level of laughter—you know what I mean, right? The kind that emotionally feels so good, but physically hurts so badly.

Day 9

After one of my run-of-the-mill days doing door-to-door soliciting... I mean *consulting*... I came back to the office and picked up the phone. Even though I never got anywhere with telemarketing calls, they made me feel like an honest worker. "Hi, this is Noelle. Can I please speak with your CFO?"

Catch this reply, "Sure, hold on one second." Say what?!

After a moment of elevator music, I hear, "Hello, this is Jeff." All of a sudden my stomach knotted up and my throat went dry.

What I tried to casually say was, "Hi Jeff. It's nice to finally get a hold of you." What came out of my parched mouth was, "Hi Jeff. It's nice to finally *get to hold you*!"

The moment the last word slipped off my tongue, I realized what I said. Simultaneously, Shellee and I fell off our chairs and laughed so hard no noises came out of us. Tears streamed down my face and I could hear Jeff saying, "Hello? Is anyone there?" At one point I screamed, because I had no control over my breathing or my vocal cords, "I am so sorry! I... just... called...." That was all I could do in my crouched position, on the floor in hysterical laughter. What did he do? He hung up.

APPLICATIONS

Heart:

It seems almost embarrassing to point out the obvious: I wasn't totally convicted in what I was doing. Yes, I had great products to sell. Yes, I was very competent at placing the right machines in the right offices. But due to my failure mentality, I wasn't actually prepared to be in the midst of an amazing opportunity. Quite honestly, that is how I lived life in general for so many years. I rarely gave thought to my deepest purpose, so I never prepared my heart for divine appointments that God put in my path.

But in your hearts set apart Christ as Lord. Always be prepared to give an answer to everyone who asks you to give the reason for the hope that you have. But do this with gentleness and respect... (1 Peter 3:15)

In your heart right now, how can you set apart Christ as Lord? The answer seems so basic, but ask yourself, "Is He above my list of things to do and above all the run-of-the-mill chaos that can take over my day?" If daily quiet times are not yet a habit, put them in your calendar and treat your time with God like an appointment. Once you have Him set apart in your heart, look at 1 Peter 3:15 again. What is the reason for the hope that you have? Do you have scriptural references to back up your statements? Rehearse the answer you wrote in your journal again and again in your mind.

Are you willing to ask God to place people in your life with whom you can share your testimony with gentleness and respect? You're created to live a big life and to share your "secrets" with others so they can live life on a grand scale too! These upcoming God-created appointments will be far more significant than a copier sales rep talking to a CFO, so be prepared... please no screaming... and please... for heaven's sake... don't tell strangers how nice it is to finally get to hold them!

Mind:

You grow up the day you have your first real laugh, at yourself.
–Ethel Barrymore

Day 9

I literally cannot count how many crazy mistakes I made at that job. I remember one of the guys whispering to Shellee, "You'd better tell Noelle her skirt is tucked into her pantyhose." I also remember the day I was running late for an appointment, so I decided to run to the office's front door in my heels. The combination of high heels, cobblestone and bad balance ended up in two bloody kneecaps which were huge eyesores busting through my black nylons (yes, I went into the appointment like that). If I tried to list all of my mistakes at that job or in life in general, it would be never-ending. The good news is that my laughter is also never-ending.

Do you have stories that bring you to that same emotion? Doesn't that feel good to be able to laugh at yourself instead of taking yourself too seriously? Proverbs 17:22 says, *"A cheerful heart is good medicine, but a crushed spirit dries up the bones."* In your journal, write out situations you are currently in where your bones feel dried up and your spirit feels broken. How can you lighten up, laugh and have a cheerful heart? This isn't a rhetorical question. Really, how can you do it? What steps can you take? Write them out in your journal. Circle one of your solutions and commit to implementing it within the next 24 hours. If you're ready for even more fun, take a bigger dose of medicine and implement each of your strategies. Get into this habit. Let's have some fun!

Body:

Speaking of being prepared, does that describe the way you approach your nutrition and fitness? In your journal, answer these questions:

Nutrition:

- What do I have in the freezer and the pantry to create quick, healthy meals on the days when I am too busy to cook?
- Do I know a couple of safe options at the restaurants where I eat? If not, when will I research their nutritional information?
- Which days/times work best for me to plan my meals for the week and which days/times work best for me to go to the market for my ingredients?
- What measures have I taken or what needs to be done to give me healthy food choices at home, school, at work and in my car?
- Am I keeping water with me so I can hydrate well?
- How can I educate myself in specific areas where I need more knowledge regarding my nutritional plan? Psst... this isn't rocket science... don't forget about Google... but stay away from sites which have claims that are too good to be true, or ones that say that you don't need to eat well or exercise.

I plan my family's meals one week at a time and I shop for my ingredients early on Saturday mornings. If I know a particular day will be extra busy, I tend to rely on my slow cooker. There are still those days when I plan a healthy meal, but due to circumstances I run out of time to cook it. On those days I open my freezer. Right now, if you were to peek inside, you'd find healthy frozen pizzas, frozen packs of brown rice and turkey meatballs. I can make a pizza, open a salad bag from the fridge and have a healthy pizza night. Or I can

Day 9

heat up the turkey meatballs, cover it with reduced-fat cream of mushroom soup and add leftover veggies. Either option is quicker, healthier and less expensive than getting take-out for my family. It's not the healthiest that we eat, but it's kid-friendly and the lesser of the evils when you consider fast food or a meal at a restaurant.

Fitness:

- Do I have my workouts scheduled into my day as irrevocable appointments with myself? If not, when can I put them into my calendar? Now! (Sorry, did I just say that? I actually meant to yell that.)
- What are my back-up plans on the days when I can't do my regular routine?
- How will I approach work traveling and vacations as an athlete?
- What added resources do I need to get me from where I am right now to my goals?

Every weekday you can find me with my boot camp team at 5:30 a.m. It's a non-negotiable appointment I make each morning. I start my day feeling physically and emotionally strong. On the days when I travel for work, I call ahead of time to find out if my hotel has a gym and what the hours are. If I can't workout at their gym before my day starts, I pack a DVD and exercise in my room. I also stash a jump rope and a resistance band inside my suitcase. When I travel, I'm still an athlete! It doesn't change my character, it just changes my location.

You know what it takes for you to be prepared... Get on it!

Day 10

I gave my parents a run for their money when I was in high school. My creative and rather brilliant (from my perspective) mind was used for things such as: keeping my spiked hair standing tall on windy days; figuring out how to use two Dixie cups and a piece of string to whisper to my friend on the other side of my algebra classroom, so technically I wasn't breaking the teacher's rules by *talking*; and doing as little school work as possible while remaining eligible to play on the basketball team.

As you can imagine, it wasn't by choice—and it certainly didn't take anyone by surprise—that I spent over two years at the local junior college before I could even apply to a four-year university. While I was in junior college, I changed my major mid-stream which added an additional semester of prerequisite classes. So, instead of transferring to the University of California at Riverside in the fall like all of the other new students, I enrolled during the winter session.

Anyone who has had to start a new school in the middle of the year can understand what it feels like to be the odd kid out. All the students had already settled into their social groups. They knew when and where to eat and who they were going to eat with. They had someone to walk through campus with to get to their lecture halls. In the evenings, the dorms were full of clusters of friends talking and laughing together... except in my room. Don't get me wrong—there was a party going on every night, but it was a pity party and there was only one party-goer.

One morning I made a commitment to stop feeling sorry for myself. I grabbed my basketball and headed to the court outside. I needed to remember my strengths instead of moping around in my insecurities. I worked on my ball handling, my jump shot and I practiced free throws with a strong follow-through. I ran sprint drills with speed and agility. Within minutes I started to regain my confidence. Ahh! A breath of fresh air. I started to remember who I was.

After a couple of hours, I went back to my room and spoke out loud, "I am changing my attitude and I'm going to be a 'glass-is-half-full' kind of girl no matter what." I decided to reward myself for taking such a positive step. In addition to my typical shower supplies, I decided to add a true piece of luxury to celebrate my victorious new mindset. The mud mask I splurged on at Christmastime was certainly a well-deserved spoiling. My arms were full with bottles of my estrogen-spiked indulgences as I headed to the showers at the end of the hall.

The stream of hot water on my back melted away my homesickness. I put on the bright blue mud mask and I could literally feel my stress levels and sadness come down in intensity. I thought my world was finally starting to rock. And then, I realized it *really* was rocking. EARTHQUAKE! I held onto both sides of the shower stall hoping the rolling waves would subside. It took all I had to keep my balance. There was a rumble of shouts and screaming in the hallway. And then the true magnitude hit me. I am naked with a fluorescent blue face and I only have a small gym towel to cover my body. Technically, I was supposed to be under the doorjamb in the hallway with the rest of the residents in this coed wing. Did you catch that? *Coed*, not *girls'* wing.

I quietly turned off the water and became as still as possible. I heard yelling. It was our Residents' Assistant (RA), "Is everyone accounted for?"

"Yes!" *Phew!* I thought. That was a close call.

Day 10

"Wait! What about the new girl?" Oh no, this wasn't heading in the direction I had hoped. "I heard someone in the shower stall... could it be her?"

"Go check!" the RA directed.

You guessed it. The next thing I knew, I was escorted out in the hallway with sudsy hair, a neon blue face and a flimsy white towel which barely covered my body. "Who is that?" a voice whispered a few doorways down. I heard laughter, but I didn't have the guts to look up and see where it came from.

Has anything like this ever happened to you? Have you ever taken a giant step to get back on the right track only to fall in a pit?

APPLICATIONS

Heart:

If the LORD delights in a man's way,
he makes his steps firm;
though he stumble, he will not fall,
for the LORD upholds him with his hand. (Psalm 37:23-24)

Certainly my steps to overcome my pity party were a delight to the Lord. Through the craziness of the earthquake and my emotional aftermath, I will be the first to admit I did stumble, but I didn't fall. I stumbled by going right back down memory lane and returning to my pity party of one. I camped there for a few more days. But I soon realized that I had a big choice to make. Would I let this stumble paralyze me? Would I be a full-time dorm hermit? Or would I let the Lord uphold me so I could regain my momentum and join the *real* party?

The stakes were actually greater than I realized at the time. What kind of representative would I have been for my faith had I gone into hiding from that day on because of a silly stumble? My knee-jerk reaction was to walk around wallowing in my misfortunes like Bad Luck Schleprock (please tell me you know the Flintstones circa 1971).

In Matthew 5:14-16, Jesus said, *"You are the light of the world. A city on a hill cannot be hidden. Neither do people light a lamp and put it under a bowl. Instead they put it on its stand, and it gives light to everyone in the house. In the same way, let your light shine before men, that they may see your good deeds and praise your Father in heaven."*

You and I are lights of the world... Get up Schleprock! For me, I've learned to laugh at my stumbles. I actually shine a light on them and get others to laugh along with me. As I met new friends in the dorm, I introduced myself by saying, "Hi, I'm the new girl Noelle with the blue face. You might not recognize me because I decided to wear clothes today." There's a sense of freedom that comes to us when we let go of perfection and instead reach up for God's hand. We are human after all. After every stumble, we have a distinct opportunity to grow in character as we grab His hand and stand back up.

Describe your most recent stumble in your journal. It can be anything such as making a bad decision at work, losing your patience with your kids, choosing to hold a grudge against your spouse, or falling off the nutritional wagon and eating a hidden stash of junk food... the possibilities are endless every day.

What steps do you need to take to stand back up? Do you need to ask for forgiveness? Should you rid your fridge, freezer and pantry of junk food? Maybe you need to redo a project at

Day 10

work. Even though it takes effort, you'll feel so amazing when you take the steps toward restoration. How can you ensure that you will reach for God's hand and let go of your pursuit of perfectionism when you stumble in the future? Write your ideas in your journal.

Mind:

Going back to basketball illustrations, check out this player's stats, "I've missed more than 9,000 shots in my career. I've lost almost 300 games. Twenty-six times, I've been trusted to take the game winning shot and missed. I've failed over and over and over again in my life. And that is why I succeed."

Hmm, what? Wait... who is this? Joe Loser Schmo? No, it's Michael Jordan, arguably the best player to ever play the game. What would have happened to the sport had he let those stumbles turn into a fall? Can you imagine the sport of basketball without the legendary name of Michael Jordan? I think we're all thankful that he took so many risks and endured the stumbles and never fell or quit. He revolutionized the game with his talent and his attitude!

Have you ever thought, "I knew I shouldn't have made myself vulnerable... I'll never do *that* again!"? You may have taken a risk and entered into a new love relationship, trusted a friend, tried out a new church for the first time or maybe you decided to completely reinvent yourself physically... but then you hit a pothole and stumbled. If you think about it logically, isn't it crazy that some of those instances can dictate a lifetime of decision making?

That attitude, which says "I'll never do *that* again," points to a notable failure in your life. What is it? You have one right? If not, call me... you'll be my first friend who is without large catastrophes. How have these failures dictated your decision making? Have you become defensive? Have you given up in certain areas of your life? How can you take that part of your life where you fell way short and turn it into Michael Jordan's quote? How will that failure turn into a great success? Journal your brainstorming.

Body:

Does this situation sound like anything you've ever experienced? You determine once and for all that you are going to get healthy. Maybe it was a New Year's resolution, or maybe it was a randomly inspired day when you drew a line in the sand. After a week or so, you hit the snooze button on your alarm clock one too many times and slept in. You rationalized this pattern for a week because your body "needed the rest" and you were going to get back on track the following Monday.

Of course, that Monday never came until the next year's New Year's resolution. And, on that line-in-the-sand moment, you either had a family member or a friend say, "Oh gosh, here you go again. You do this every year. Let's just fast forward to February first and save the money on the gym dues."

Or, maybe there are no nay-sayers in your life, but you hear those thoughts in your head. Don't forget, you have a real adversary. He just happens to be invisible to our human eyes. Of course it's normal to have those thoughts in your head. But it is not mandatory to agree with them. In fact, you need to stand firm against the devil who would love nothing more than to have you live in an unfit body with a poor self-image.

Day 10

Dust yourself off and reach for God's hand if you have stumbled. Call someone immediately who will let God work through him or her to pick you up. Maybe it's a friend, maybe it's a personal trainer, or maybe you need to get online and find a support group. If this applies to you now, journal your action steps and check it off upon completion. If this doesn't apply to you, chances are good it will at some point, so proactively journal your plan for those times when you will stumble.

Day 11

My Mom listened to her oncologist as he described the effects the chemotherapy would have on her cancer-ridden body. Although her surgeon had told us she would die within a year, our first meeting with Dr. Barth gave us a new outlook. He had the same message... there wasn't a cure for metastatic colon cancer per se... but he explained the tumor-killing capability of her weekly infusions with an air of confidence. If she could just "tread water," there was always a chance that there would be a cure around the corner. The reason we sat in his office in the first place was because we had heard of his innovative ways of approaching otherwise bleak prognoses, and we were desperate for any ray of hope. Our hope did come with a price tag though, which were the accompanying side effects of nausea, vomiting, diarrhea and hair loss.

To know my Mom is to know the loveliest warrior. She was a delicate balance of beauty and fierceness. You'd assume she would have shown some sign of anger, devastation or fear as she was being counseled on her upcoming battle. But with a smile, she clasped her hands together and said, "I'm okay. I am going to fight this. It's actually harder to be in your shoes," as she looked at my Dad, Lori and me. "You want to take this burden from me, but you can't, so you feel helpless."

Through the first few treatments, she had almost every adverse event that she was warned about. The nausea and vomiting would start in the middle of her infusion and last for several days. She kept hair for the first few months since hair loss is a cumulative toxicity reaction, but you could still see changes in its texture. The one side effect we were highly cautioned about specific to this particular chemotherapy was diarrhea. I felt like I had become the president of Bowel Movements R Us. Every time I called her, I'd ask if there were any "movement changes" right after saying, "Hi Mom." Oddly enough, she never had the problem. She told Dr. Barth, "It's the Japanese rice! It can plug anything up. You should tell your other patients about it!"

I decided to visit my Mom in the middle of my workday after her third infusion. When I visited my parents' home, I used my key instead of ringing the doorbell. I thought I heard my Mom in her room, so I made my way back through the hallways. The door was cracked open and I caught a glimpse of her tiny body. That vision still puts an ache in my heart today. She was carefully collecting the hair on her pillow that had come off her head while she slept. The chemo had built up enough in her system so that her hair was coming out in patches. She didn't notice my presence, so I stood briefly and watched. Tears streamed down her cheeks and within seconds, she was weeping out loud.

"Oh Mom..." was all I could think to say. Surprised by my presence, she quickly wiped the tears from her eyes and said, "I'm sorry Noey. Give me a day to mourn and I'll be back fighting tomorrow."

I certainly hope that in my lifetime, cancer treatments will advance to the point where we will look back on chemotherapy and say, "Remember how barbaric that was?" Because although it kills the cancer cells, it's so toxic it also damages the good cells. When you think about it, that's no different than how our hearts, minds and bodies are affected by toxicity. If we feed our hearts with negativity, our minds with self-defeating thoughts or our bodies with processed junk, the toxic effects will take over.

Day 11

APPLICATIONS

Heart:

Do you have toxic messages in your heart? If you do, would you even know it? I mean, how many of us would even consider taking an inventory of what is in our hearts?

A few days ago, we learned that we are at war. Maybe that was a new concept to you, maybe not. Well, the enemy in this war has been working overtime to damage your heart. Think about it. The worse the condition of your heart, the smaller capacity for you to know God and the less effective you will be. The deceiver can work through harsh words people have spoken to you. He can also do unspeakable damage through horrific abuse which has led you to believe you are not worthy of love. His tactics are endless. Chances are good your heart is holding a fair amount of toxicity due to lies you believe about yourself. I grew up thinking I wasn't smart since people unknowingly categorized my sister as the "smart one" and I was the "athletic one." I never expected anything of myself and I wasn't using any of the gifts God placed in my soul. Man, how those hurtful messages stung! Mind you, I grew up in a safe and loving home. I can't begin to imagine the damage for those of you who didn't have that type of built-in safety.

"For as he thinks in his heart, so is he..." (Proverbs 23:7 NKJ)

In this Proverb, we see someone who is two-faced. His outer actions were impressive, but he wasn't that person. We see who he really was by what he was thinking in his heart. Did you catch that? We become what we think in our hearts!

Transformation by Truth

This is a huge caps lock, underlined point! So, where do we go from here? Ask God to reveal the toxicity that is clouding your heart. You, probably unconsciously, made agreements with the deceitful thoughts the devil was putting in your heart, and you became those lies. Ask God to reveal the lies that have become a part of your heart and write them out one by one in your journal. Consider the messages that were given to you verbally, through someone's actions and by circumstances. In Jesus' Name, ask for each of those ties to be broken and ask God to fill your heart with His love and truth.

If you are having a hard time hearing God's truth over the enemy's lies, here is a small sampling of what God says specifically about you. Look up the verses. Journal at least one verse that applies to your struggle. Place it where you will see it often and commit it to memory.

You are:
God's son or daughter (John 1:12)
Jesus' friend (John 15:15)
Justified and redeemed (Romans 3:24)
Not condemned (Romans 8:1)
Set free from the law of sin and death (Romans 8:2)
Accepted by Jesus (Romans 15:7)
Called to be a saint (1 Corinthians 1:2)
A new creature in Jesus (Galatians 3:28)
Chosen, holy and blameless before God (Ephesians 1:4)
Redeemed and forgiven by grace (Ephesians 1:7)
God's workmanship (Ephesians 2:10)
Now light, though you were once in darkness (Ephesians 5:8)

Day 11

Mind:

Finally, brothers, whatever is true, whatever is noble, whatever is right, whatever is pure, whatever is lovely, whatever is admirable—if anything is excellent or praiseworthy—think about such things. (Philippians 4:8)

Do you ever get stuck in a trap thinking, "I can't help what is in my mind... there are toxic thoughts, but what can I do about it?" There's no doubt that the enemy will put poisonous messages in your mind. But guess who has the control to either agree with it or dismiss it? That's right—you! Even if you can't completely wipe out the contaminated thoughts, you can proactively feed your mind. Re-read Philippians 4:8 above. Write in your journal the types of things we should think about and explain what this looks like on a practical level in your life using specific examples.

Now, let me ask you this... what's on your iPod? What programs are you watching on TV? What are you reading? Who do you talk to during your day? What do you listen to when you're driving? These are the things you are proactively filling your mind with. Are they noble, pure, lovely, admirable, excellent and praiseworthy? I had to completely change what I kept on my iPod. If I didn't know the lyrics, I researched it online. Hello conviction! But now, wherever I am, I feed my mind with awesome music, sermons, motivational talks and great reading. I also know that certain people can be toxic. I limit my conversations with them as much as possible and keep the content upbeat. What can you do today and from now on to keep your mind free of toxicity? Journal your responses and put them into action!

Transformation by Truth

Body:

Think about your food and drinks not only as joy, but also as fuel for your body. Are you filling your tank mainly with clean-burning fuel? Or are you running on toxins? Going back to the 80-20 plan, let's take a deeper look at the 80 percent of what you are eating. Someone asked me a few days ago what I meant when I talk about "whole foods" or "clean eating." My reply was a question about the food they eat, "Did it have a mom or did it grow from the ground?" The less processed our food, the better. There is a monumental difference between processed food which has an entire paragraph of ingredients you cannot pronounce compared to whole, clean food. Eating clean makes a difference in your metabolism, it aids in your energy level and helps you achieve and maintain a healthy weight.

Take a look at what you have on hand. Break out a Hefty trash bag and toss the junk food items that you know are stumbling blocks for you. I know, I know. You can't because there are starving children in third world countries. Well, throwing away your poor food choices will not affect them. Ditch your junk and donate money to help those children. Yes, I do eat a treat every single day, but that does not mean I need a bag of Oreos in the pantry. When you open my freezer, you will find my favorite frozen yogurt. If something is going to cause you to binge, keep it on the shelves of the store, not in your home. If you really want it, drive and pick up a single serving. Your environment should be mainly toxin free. Google the terms: "healthy pantry items," "healthy freezer items" and "healthy refrigerator." Honk if you hate toxins!

"But I don't have the time to eat well." Yeesh! Give me a break. If you have your environment stocked up and if you

Day 11

plan your meals, it will take you less time to whip up healthy, yummy meals and snacks than it would to hit a greasy drive thru. Google "fast healthy meals" and there will be pages upon pages of awesome ideas. Journal your favorite ideas and implement them into your lifestyle from here on. Not only will you feel better and attain or maintain a healthy weight, but you'll also save money on the pink goopy medicine you would have had to guzzle once indigestion hit... and you won't have to see your psychologist for all the guilt-related issues that inevitably would have followed the morning after. Wow... with all the money and time you'll be saving, do you want to take me out to lunch? Sushi please!

Day 12

I woke up early on our first day in Lake Tahoe so I could officially begin my summer vacation with a mountain bike ride. There was a mile-and-a-half climb up Heavenly Valley's ski run that was calling my name. I don't bike nearly as much as you'd guess given how nice my bike is. But on the rare times when I suit up, I do what I can to ride on my husband's coattail. Ryan always looks hot (not as in temperature) with his bike gear: his helmet is sleek and it goes with his Oakley sunglasses. His cycle jersey shows off his body and the CamelBak water pack he wears is flat out cool.

And then there's me. Ryan and I have an ongoing joke about my helmet since my head is bigger than his. Of course I argue that a big head means a big brain. Ryan lovingly explains, "It's the crown of your head that's so big. It's not your whole head." Whatever. For those of you who are anywhere near my age, you might remember Gazoo from the Flintstones. If you have no idea what I'm talking about, it's worth the visual. Use Google Images and search under "Gazoo Flintstones." When you see the alien with his oversized head and helmet, you'll get the picture.

So, there I was: 5'3" Japanese Gazoo girl with a big, round helmet (I couldn't find an aerodynamic one in my size), mismatched cycle gear and although I used one of Ryan's CamelBaks, I didn't know how to strap it on correctly. So, I looked like I was giving a piggy back ride to an orangutan who wrapped its arms and legs around my body desperately trying to hold on.

Transformation by Truth

As you can imagine, I was more than a little self-conscious wondering what people who saw me might have thought, as if they cared. When I walked from our hotel to where my bike was, I already felt the effects of the high altitude. I also realized my clothes weren't nearly warm enough for the cold Lake Tahoe morning. Nonetheless, I ventured out and started my climb. To my dismay, I went so slow that I had to steer just to avoid falling.

The grade got steeper and I could feel the burning in my legs. I literally obsessed over that pain. My breathing was heavy and my teeth chattered from the cold. I knew that if a little grandma was out walking her toy poodle, she would have been able to pass me. Those were the types of visions that were trapped in my mind. Although it crushed my confidence, I had to stop not once but twice before I reached the top of the hill.

I eventually reached my finish line, but I knew that this hill and my lack of belief would plague me all day long. A fierce fire burned inside me, so I rode back to the base of the hill. I refused to start pedaling until I could flawlessly run a movie in my mind. In the movie, I looked incredibly athletic. My muscles were well-defined. My face showed resilience and tenacity. The stride and pace I held would make Lance Armstrong give me a second glance. The helmet? Well, I couldn't do much with that.

Anyhow, the only other visualizations I would allow in my mind during the steep climb were pictures of people on the sidelines cheering me on to victory. In between my breaths, I would tell myself, "I'm an athlete!" I'm sure you already know the end of the story: I finished without stopping once. The next morning I climbed the hill twice. I didn't just complete the rides without stopping, but I improved my

Day 12

time by a handful of minutes. What a difference that shift of perspective made!

APPLICATIONS

Heart:

Jesus looked at them and said, "With man this is impossible, but with God all things are possible." (Matthew 19:26)

I'm not a "name-it-and-claim-it" kind of girl, but I use my biking story to illustrate the difference between belief and unbelief. When I was climbing with unbelief, I was obsessively focused on my pain and everything that was going awry. But after I regrouped and put my mind in a believing mode, it changed everything. All of a sudden, I had hope. The center of my attention was triumphant victory. I still endured physical pain, but the outcome and my joy in the two climbs were completely different... all due to the discipline of belief.

What... or better said... *who*... dictates your belief? Here's what I mean: I'm a strong girl. On a physical level, I have power and stamina. Emotionally, I've endured a fair amount of hardship, but I've made it through seemingly unscathed. The Noelle that the world sees is strong enough to put your belief in. But at the end of the day, I'm not the Noelle that everyone thinks I am... I'm just a girl!

There were only a few people who knew that my parents' deaths caused me to have panic attacks. I hide my insecurities and frailties as best as I can. Only God and I know how weak I am inside. The truth is, it doesn't take much to wear me down. Hurtful words, a rough day at work, relational struggles, financial instability, being faced with tragedies... any one of these things can crush me inside. So when my belief is only being dictated by me and my abilities, I have no basis to really believe.

Re-read Matthew 19:26. There are two opposing statements. One parallels my first bike ride and the other is similar to my second ride. Understanding that you and I are "man," does it look like we are built to be a Superman or Wonderwoman? So what is the true key to unlocking all possibilities? What does that look like in your life? Journal your response.

Understanding that, let's dig in. What is in your heart of hearts? Do you have dreams that you continue to deny because those types of dreams are for others who appear to have their lives all together? Heaven knows you're not as strong as others think you are, right? I used to have thoughts pound inside my mind that would say, "Why would God want that for *you*? Dreams of that magnitude are for the brilliant and the righteous... and newsflash... neither of those adjectives adorn your résumé!" But... what if your deepest desires were God-authored? Matthew 19:26 says if it only depended on you, those dreams would be impossible. But look at the second half of the verse. With God, how many things are possible?

So what is in your heart of hearts? Freedom from addiction? Joy regardless of circumstances? A healthy, lean body? What is it? Look at the promise we have when our desires are in line with God's will...

This is the confidence we have in approaching God: that if we ask anything according to his will, he hears us. And if we know that he

Day 12

hears us—whatever we ask—we know that we have what we asked of him. (1 John 5:14-15)

Journal your dreams... get specific. What will you do today to know you have what you have asked of Him according to His will? Write your plan!

Mind:

I once heard Joyce Meyer explain that God caused her to look at Matthew 19:26 in a different light. She already knew that God was more than capable of doing the impossible. And although she read that verse many times before, for the first time she felt the Holy Spirit point out a practical lesson to the second part of the verse. If it *is* possible with man, that is *our* job!

One of my biggest life dreams has been to write a book and have it published. What would have happened if I waited on God like He was the Tooth Fairy? Would my book ever be written? Of course not! Yes, I believe that God will provide what I need to make my project come together. And yes, I believe He will use my book in people's lives to bring healing through the words He inspired me to write. But at the same time, I've set aside time each day to write and I have researched what it takes to get my work published. I'm committed to doing what is possible for me to do and I know that God will do what I can't.

When you look at your journaled dream(s), what components of your dreams are possible for you to take action on? Journal each step you can take that is within your capabilities. What is your timeline for each task? List it out and do your part!

Transformation by Truth

Body:

Your belief determines your action and your action determines your results, but first you have to believe. —Mark Victor Hansen

Do you know exactly what your body will look like once you hit your fitness goals? I'm talking about *your* body... not someone else's. I admire J-Lo's body, but I can wish and hope 'til the cows come home and I will never have a single one of her curves. So here's what *my* body looks like at its best: my shoulders show muscle definition as do my legs; my abs never sport a six pack, but my hips and glutes are solid. How about yours?

Once you get that picture in your mind, on a scale from one to ten, where is your belief? Do you think that you can achieve that body? When you can believe it... I mean when you feel it in your blood... you start to take the action that goes along with that body.

The physique I saw in my mind was incredibly athletic. So my workouts and eating became consistent with that outcome. I started taking classes at the gym. Mountain bike riding, rollerblading and hiking became pastimes I looked forward to. I found out how athletes fueled their bodies.

Of course, when you put in that kind of work, the outcome is no mystery. But as Mark Victor Hansen points out, "...first you have to believe." If you were anything short of ten on your rating, list the steps you need to take to get your mind up to a ten in belief. Start believing and doing what is in your power. Once your belief is secured, go attack your workouts. You are an athlete. Don't let that visual slip from your mind during any part of your workout. If it does, refocus and lock that picture back in your mind. Get aggressive!

Day 13

I had no idea just how good I had it in college. My parents paid for all of my tuition, dorm expenses, books and food. My Dad, in his infinite wisdom, only required that I submit a budget of my expenses. This budget needed to meet his approval. My first one got rejected because I was informed that ten dollars per week was not a wise food allowance even if Top Ramen was only a buck for ten. After my budget was okayed, my Dad would deposit that exact amount into my checking account.

The only things I had to pay for were my clothes, entertainment and meals out. For a college kid, those were bare necessities, so I set out to find a job. Some of my friends worked in nearby offices while others drove a few miles to work in retail shops at the mall. As for me, my shoes were my car; so my only option for money making was on school grounds. One application sufficed for all on-campus jobs. The good news: they hired me. The bad news: they stuck me in the dorm's cafeteria.

I was embarrassed by the thought of serving up food to the same people I lived with since I was already humbled by the earthquake incident. But, little did I know, my embarrassment would soon escalate to a whole new level. My first day on the job actually started out great. When I went downstairs to the cafeteria, I distinctly remember thinking, "Well, at least I look cool in my faded 501 jeans and my worn-in t-shirt." It seemed to get even better when the manager welcomed me with a warm smile and my coworkers walked up and introduced themselves. Wow! Maybe that job was sent from heaven. Maybe its purpose was to help me make friends. And then? Insert suspenseful music here. In fact, insert the musical score for the movie *Jaws*.

The smiling manager excitedly said, "You are starting at a great time! This is International Week and today is Oriental Day!" After that, he handed me a pile of what I thought was a white bed sheet on top of a wicker basket. Strike that thought. It was a white kimono-like robe and a huge straw rice paddy hat. "Everyone get dressed up! Let's get this party going!"

Okay. I realized I had self-esteem issues. What I wouldn't have done to return to my high school days where I was MVP on the varsity basketball team as a freshman and where I was voted prom princess and class clown as a senior. No, this was a new world. And, let's be real. If you have a handful of good looking white people in these types of get-ups, it looks like a Halloween prank. But, if you are Asian, you don't know a soul and you are wearing a kimono with a wide cone-shaped straw hat so big you have to keep your feet apart and bend at your knees to maintain your equilibrium (heaven forbid I had to turn my head while I scooped up clumps of white sticky rice and broccoli beef), well... that's just plain wrong.

Years later my Dad explained that it pained him to hear my stories. He had enough money to pay for all my expenses and he truly felt sorry for me. I thought he was kidding, but when I realized he wasn't, I asked, "If that's true, why did you make me endure the humiliation? Would it have killed you to give me an extra 20 dollars a week? Where was your compassion?"

In a soft voice and in all seriousness he explained, "It was times like those when true, unshakeable character was born.

Day 13

What you viewed as a tragedy, a failure, even humiliation gave birth to a humble spirit based on gratitude."

APPLICATIONS

Heart:

Trust in the LORD with all your heart and lean not on your own understanding; in all your ways acknowledge him, and he will make your paths straight. (Proverbs 3:5-6)

When I was scooping up food in the cafeteria, I never put thought into what my Dad's intentions were for my personal growth. I judged his character based on my own understanding. As I matured, I realized the brilliance and depths of love in which my Dad founded his decisions. He was an incredibly humble, patient, generous and loving man. If anything, I feel honored every time someone tells me I take after him. I also thank God for my cafeteria days which have helped shape who I have become.

Are you living through difficult times right now? Write about your challenges in your journal. Have you ever wondered why God doesn't swoop you out of these hardships? Do you catch yourself thinking, "How could a loving God let this happen to me?" Stop and pause for a moment.

Now look at your situation from the perspective of being the parent. God is your Heavenly Father... your loving Daddy... What good can come from your taxing circumstances? Are there specific character traits you see emerging? In your journal, write out the life lessons your Daddy might be teaching you. Then, reply to that wisdom by journaling the steps you will implement this very moment to grow your character.

Transformation by Truth

Mind:

Those words my Dad spoke to me where incredibly powerful, "...true, unshakeable character..." Doesn't that sum up what you strive for? How can you attain it? You can start by putting your life's mission statement into words. Words hold creative power. How do you complete the phrase, "I'm the kind of person who..."? Write it from the perspective of who you strive to be. Once you create your mission statement, keep it with you somewhere so you can read it often and revise as needed. My most current mission statement looks like this:

I am a fierce warrior for truth. I seek God first and foremost and love living life on this edgy plane of deep faith. I am Ryan's wife. I not only love my husband to crazy extents, but I'm a wife who keeps my marriage flirtatious, silly, compassion-filled, and I don't keep a score of rights and wrongs. I love being Sierra's Mommy. I'm the kind of Mom who listens to the details of her daughter's stories. I know each one of her imaginary friends and her dreams to be an archeologist. I am a dedicated employee who brings hope to cancer patients by effectively communicating solutions to their doctors. I'm the kind of person who will fight the good fight. I strive for the best, but I don't get caught up in the boring world of perfection. I protect my friends. I will lead others to find the amazing joy and faith I live with each day. I am a competitive athlete. I love to workout and eat clean, but I never live a day without enjoying a favorite treat. I play aggressively to win; I never play defensively. I'm the kind of person who looks for opportunities to be someone's angel. And, I wouldn't be me if I didn't look for ways to drive people crazy. I am the daughter of God Himself, and I celebrate my God-given life!

Day 13

Did you realize that you get to create your own character? You mission statement will inspire you... test it out and see!

Body:

What kind of an athlete are you? What did it say in your mission statement? How would you finish this sentence, "I'm the kind of athlete who..."? Once you create and begin to live your athletic, healthy characteristics, it's not stressful to maintain "a plan." Being active and eating well will just be a way of life. If you believe that you are in fact a fierce athlete no matter what your body looks like now, you will start to live like one. You'll eat like one, you'll train like one. So, ask yourself point blank: are you living off of willpower or is health and wellness integrated into your character?

I have had numerous clients tell me it's crazy to call themselves athletes. Believe me, I've heard it all, "I'm fat and middle-aged." "I've never played a sport in my entire life." "I was always chosen last by the team captains in grade school." Okay. That was then, this is now. What would God say? Do you think He'd say, "All things are possible with God... hmm... well... I mean all things except your weight loss... and all things minus you becoming an athlete..." I'm pretty sure "all" means "all."

During your workout today, replay your athletic mission statement in your mind. Finish the statement, "I'm the kind of athlete who..." in your journal. Keeping in line with that mission, what are you eating today? How will you hydrate? Make sure it fits within your healthy character. If it doesn't, mark my words, you'll feel "off." It's a matter of character, not willpower!

Day 14

The moment you'd walk into a room, you would have known if my Mom was there or not. She had a laugh that sounded like two parts hyena mixed with one part rooster cackle. Once you heard her contagious laughter, you would be greeted by her gorgeous smile. It didn't matter if you knew her for years or whether you were meeting her for the first time... you would instantly feel like family. Margaret Sase was always the life of the party and she had a heart of compassion that drew you close.

Our family was eating at the Crab Cooker one night and a family behind us was having their orders taken. You could hear the struggle in the server's voice as he attempted to break the language barrier with his Hispanic customers. Fortunately for the server, my non-Spanish-speaking Mom felt his pain and was there to help. As she stood up from our table, my Dad, Lori and I all pleaded, "Mom, no!" But, with her dashing smile, she stood next to the server, doing her best charade of a crab. Her hands turned into pinching claws and she rolled her "R's" to (loudly) say "Crrrrrrrabs (because when someone doesn't understand you, it's always best to create an accent and increase your volume, right?). Do you want crrrrrrabs?!" Notice: no Spanish words were spoken. We all sunk down into our booth hoping no one realized that Japanese woman belonged to us... the only Japanese family in the restaurant.

And that was just one of many stories. There was also the Laguna Beach fire in 1993 that burned 366 homes and 17,000 acres. A police car drove slowly up and down our street mandating immediate evacuation. We all leaned on my Dad for his wisdom and direction. But when we looked to our pillar, we found him scurrying, putting his entire drawer of socks into his suitcase and nothing else! So, it was my Mom who ended up taking the reins, "Come on Richard... hurry Noelle... grab your things and get into the car. Don't worry; I have all of our important stuff!" I caught a glimpse of her in my panic and saw that she had our dog Missy on a leash, so I assumed she truly did have all of the important things covered. After we drove away and went to the emergency relocation area, we were able to see what she brought with clearer minds. The "most important stuff" happened to be our dog and her box of coupons.

That gregarious personality and her brilliant smile were her signature, even after her metastatic colon cancer diagnosis. I would routinely drive her to chemo appointments and, as I looked in the passenger seat, I saw that her body had become so tiny, so weak. She'd close her eyes, hoping the nausea would pass, but instead of admitting her misery, she'd say to me, "I wonder if Toni will be there today. Toni needs encouragement because her battle has been so difficult. Or, maybe I'll see John. You know he just started treatments and he needs to know that he'll be okay." My Mom had become the light of her doctor's office. And, even in her last two weeks of life, she'd hallucinate and wake up in the middle of the night saying, "Noelle! Hurry... you need to take care of Dad and get him to his doctor's appointment." As always, her heart was not self-consumed, but it was focused on giving compassion and aid to others.

One of the best pieces of advice I was given years ago was to have an altruistic mission in addition to my personal goals. This leads to higher levels of success for a couple of reasons. First, it drives us to be better human beings. Having the

Day 14

heart of generosity always goes hand-in-hand with true victory. The less obvious reason for this wisdom is that it teaches us to give grace to ourselves. When we hold others' goals in high regard, it forces us to step outside of our own world and see things from their perspectives. In doing so, we flex our compassionate, grace-filled muscles. And when those muscles are strengthened, we can then use them for ourselves! When was the last time you gave compassion and grace to yourself? You are on a unique journey... a journey that will have bumps in the road, a journey where you will make mistakes. If you can give grace to yourself and to others, not only will you enjoy the process of growing your heart, mind and body, but success and joy will consume you!

APPLICATIONS

Heart:

Do you ever have thought patterns that sound something like this: *I can give grace and compassion to others because they deserve it, but quite honestly, you have no idea how ugly I can be inside*? Messages like this swim in my mind often, and it has affected the way I have lived the majority of my life. When you take a step back, it's pretty plain to see the source of those thoughts. The enemy would love for you and me to believe his lies and to keep us from understanding who we are to God. If this speaks to your heart at all, read the story of the prodigal son in Luke 15:11-32. If you don't have a Bible, there are free online Bibles. I use www.biblegateway.com.

The son disrespectfully tells his Dad that he wants his inheritance while his Dad is still alive. Can you imagine how devastating that would be if you were the parent? Then the son runs away and squanders all of his money being reckless and wild. Okay... I don't know about you, but I've certainly had times in my life where those words can describe my choices. After he runs out of money (consider how much reckless living it took to run out of inheritance money), he feels absolutely worthless and hopes that his Dad would take him in as an employee, not a son. So, how does his Dad respond? Does he rightfully turn his back on him? That's what he deserved, right? Not even close! He sees his son in the distance, runs to him, showers him with hugs, kisses, gifts and throws a party because his son returned to him. This story is a parable where you are the prodigal son and God is your Dad.

Let's have a feast and celebrate. For this son of mine was dead and is alive again; he was lost and is found.' So they began to celebrate. (Luke 15:23-24)

This is who you are to God. What are the deepest regrets you have and the biggest mistakes you have made? They might be so big and so numerous that you don't even want to seek eye contact with God. Whatever they are, write them out in your journal. These have been weighing so heavily on your heart and you need to release them. Guess what? God already knows all about these things, and He couldn't love you more! Now picture Jesus running to you. With your head down in shame, you mumble words asking Him for forgiveness. And, as you do, he picks you up in a huge hug; He kisses your cheeks and celebrates because you have come home. He's throwing you a huge party!

What will it take for you to understand that you have been forgiven and you are released of those burdens? Are you

Day 14

now able to give a huge measure of grace to yourself? If not, how does that relate to your pride? In other words, if God forgives you, are you saying that your standards are higher and greater than His? Whoa! Catch that. We aren't being martyrs and we're certainly not being humble when we can't give grace and forgiveness to ourselves. That is a red flag that signifies pride. In your journal, re-read your list of regrets and mistakes. Write a love letter to God explaining how you are going to graciously accept His forgiveness and, in response, how you will give grace to yourself.

Make a commitment today to always join the party, no matter what mistakes you make on your journey. Commit to give yourself grace no matter what. Follow God's lead and believe His word!

Mind:

We used to make fun of my Mom because when we would be amongst others, you could tell that she was secretly nosing around to see if anyone needed her help. The funny thing is, now, Ryan routinely catches me as I gravitate toward strangers who might need me to lend a hand. Apparently I've become the embarrassing Japanese woman.

The awe I have with my Mom, though, is based on her fight against colon cancer. Even when she was in the ultimate struggle for her life, my Mom still had a heart for wanting others to succeed in their own battles. I used to wonder if she would have been better off solely concentrating on taking care of herself and pursuing her survival. But what I found was that her gracious, compassionate spirit was the reason she had an incredible depth of joy and fulfillment in her life.

Think of at least one person who could use your heart today. Write their name in your journal and explain why God has weighed that person on your mind. Take a compassionate action step before the day is through to let them know that you are firmly standing behind them in love.

Body:

Dedicate some of your life to others. Your dedication will not be a sacrifice. It will be an exhilarating experience because it is an intense effort applied toward a meaningful end. –Dr. Thomas Dooley

Make today's workout a dedication workout. Think of someone whose load you would gladly carry to give them rest. How many times have you wanted to do something for someone, but there really wasn't anything you could do? Visualize that individual as you exercise. See their victory in your mind. Dedicate your strength and endurance to them.

Why? One amazing way to honor their life is to be the best *you* that you can possibly be. So, dedication workouts are a productive way to give something special of yourself. It's like saying, "Jump on my back and ride on my strength. Let me carry you. I have you covered." When I do my dedication workouts, I tend to run faster and longer… I lift heavier weights… because I am warrior fighting on their behalf. And you? You know darn well it's who you are… you are the kind of person who fights the good fight!

End of Week Two:

The Biggest Winner!

One of the only things I don't like about NBC's show, *The Biggest Loser* is its name. Aside from that, I have to admit, I'm a junkie. Isn't it amazing to watch the contestants drop so much weight in the confines of one week? People ask me all the time, "Isn't that unrealistic?" Of course it is... unless you have six to eight hours a day to dedicate to your workouts and unless you have an elite team of trainers, physicians, life coaches and physical therapists at your beck and call. You don't? Hmm. That's weird. Kidding.

I think the show's bigger intent is to show us the capabilities of the human body, mind and heart. Certainly if they can lose 50 percent of their body weight... if they can be morbidly obese and still train with the world's toughest trainers and thrive in those intense workouts and completely overhaul their lives... it must be possible for you to fit back into your skinny jeans. Almost everyone loves a makeover story, right?

But, have you noticed how notoriously difficult the second week is for the contestants? Some of you are saying, "I don't watch the show! Enough of this already!" Bear with me. This might give you needed perspective on the week you just finished. The contestants eat the same and train the same, if not better, than they did the first week, but typically with far fewer results. Why the heck is that?

Chances are good that their bodies were so conditioned to live *years* in an unhealthy lifestyle. Then out of nowhere, they turned their lives around 180 degrees. The first week their bodies let go of a lot of excess weight. For their bodies, it wasn't worrisome because they still had a tremendous amount of excess stored energy in the form of body fat. But the second week their bodies said something like this, "Whoa! Doesn't my person know that they are losing all of this stored energy? What if I need it in the case of famine? Uh-oh. Maybe I should hang onto this extra body fat for survival. Slow down thyroid! Slow down metabolism!"

So, what do the contestants do? Well, what we see from watching the show… as I speak for us groupies… they keep going. They don't lose sight of their goals or what it takes to make it happen. Since they are being fed (I understand they have brilliant minds watching their nutrition), their bodies begin to trust the process and they start losing weight again.

This may have happened to you. You may have worked hard this week to overhaul your heart, mind and body, but for some reason you don't see the results you had hoped for. If that's the case, first check and see if there were areas where you fell off track. Maybe you did… if so, be happy you know what went wrong because that means you have a controllable solution. But if you know you did everything you could and you are lacking results, this is a defining moment for you. Trust the process. God wants you to have crazy success! He has plans to prosper you, not to harm you (Jeremiah 29:11). Keep on keepin' on! *Psst…* Don't forget to reward yourself for this second week!

Day 15

Do you ever feel like you are caught on a habitrail wheel... like your life is stuck on Groundhog's Day? Our family had been on that cycle in 2009. But instead of a groundhog, it was a *hound* dog. The year before, we laughed (kind of... well not really) over the irony that our pain-in-the-rear dog got a pain in his rear in the form of anal gland cancer. A year passed, he was still our pain in the tuchus and unfortunately, the pain in his tuchus had recurred. After another surgery, Sake had recovered, but we weren't sure if we had. Our lives, which should have revolved around first grade, revolved around stool softeners (for Sake, not for us... at least not yet).

That's right... *stool softeners*. He needed two per meal. Translation: a heck of a lot. Our budget was already tight but we made it work by purchasing generic pills and we bought in bulk. So, as you can imagine, I was far from thrilled when I picked the short straw and became the generic-stool-softener-in-bulk buyer. But there's typically something good that comes out of every story. Here was the positive side to my drug buying: I found the path of least embarrassment. If I shopped before my 5:30 a.m. workout, I could use the self-checkout at CVS and get back to my van before anyone saw the transaction.

I arrived at 4:50 a.m., got the bottle of 400 capsules and hustled to the self-checkout computers. Right before I scanned it, I was stopped in my tracks. The computer screen read, "Closed." Panicked, I turned to the other terminal, "Closed." Uh-oh. Plan B. I searched the aisles for Lisa, the sweet cashier who I typically saw on those early mornings. Since I was a regular customer at that odd hour, I had gotten to know her well and I enjoyed our conversations. She was nowhere to be found. But instead, a guy who I had never seen before quickly hollered out, "Be right there to ring you up!"

Before he could say another word, I blurted out, "Just so you know, my dog recently had surgery and these are for him. Not that you need to know, but now you know."

He got eye contact with me and said, "I'm not here to judge you. It doesn't matter who these are for."

"I know you're not here to judge me, but these are really for my dog."

"Like I said ma'am, it doesn't matter. I keep all things confidential."

I could audibly hear myself mumbling all the way to my van, "Oh my heaven. He thinks they're for me." For the first 45 minutes of my hour workout, it was all I could focus on.

As much as I'd like to pretend that others' opinions are meaningless to me, I realize I would only be fooling myself. That's why I get such a kick out of Ryan and Sierra. Ryan's motto is, "Observe the masses, and do the opposite." To know Ryan is to know a man who follows God's lead, not society's. Throughout his life, he hasn't just taken the path less traveled, but it's more like he travels the path only God and Ryan together can blaze. When others roll their eyes, he keeps on truckin'.

Little Sierra has taken after her Daddy. She couldn't have cared less when we thought her pink and white polka dotted tights didn't go well with her orange flowered shirt as she marched into her first-grade classroom. She was completely unfazed that her two front teeth were missing and her bottom teeth had yet to show up. She would run around carefree and topless when it got above 70 degrees. She continues to be clueless when she's the only one laughing at her own joke. Sierra knows God delights in her and, as for now, that's all she needs.

Day 15

How blessed I am to be living with two undeniable role models! In the same manner, I do my best to follow their lead and ignore society's grumbling. Instead I aim to hear God's voice above all. The headlines these days read, "Recession!" But in our family, we find ourselves living in the most amazing abundance. Our blessings are crazy! Maybe it hasn't translated into money, but it takes just one look at our lives to see that God's economy is obviously completely upside down compared to this world's. We are rich with our family, friendships, laughter and undying love. God versus society. We choose God.

APPLICATIONS

Heart:

I once had the opportunity to walk into the Los Angeles Angels' baseball stadium when there were no fans; it was just an empty stadium. I daydreamed about running the bases with a huge crowd roaring and cheering me on. The thought of that still gets my adrenaline pumping. And then I felt like God weighed this thought on my heart, "If I was the only fan, occupying just one seat, would you run just as hard?"

The power of *One*. Consider the power of One when you read the story of Abraham and Sarah in Genesis 17:15-19. God told Abraham at the age of 99 that he and Sarah were going to have a son. This is after Sarah's extensive heartache of infertility and the regret of having her first son through a surrogate. When their son would be born, Abraham would be 100 years old and Sarah would be 90. What do you think the buzz was in their community? "Hey Abraham, are you standing on a loose board? Oh, that's your bones creaking? And you have the nerve to say you're having a son? Dementia, my friend, dementia." "Sarah, come on now sister. You? A mom? You haven't been a spring chicken for a good half century now. Speaking of spring chickens, do you have enough teeth to eat one?" But after they both laughed, they realized this was God speaking. Abraham knew the power of One. (His name was Abram before God changed his name to Abraham, and Sarah was previously Sarai.)

Abram believed the LORD, and he credited it to him as righteousness. (Genesis 15:6)

Do you have God-given passions in your heart that others have shunned? Or maybe there's hidden desires that you're afraid to share with others. I was such a flake in high school, so when I decided to really work hard in college, I didn't tell anyone, because I figured they'd say something like, "Oh yeah. I'll believe that when I see it."

What about you? Journal your thoughts. How can you turn society's volume down and tune in only to your audience of One? Brainstorm the obstacles that you will face. Next to each obstacle, write your solution which is between you and God alone. How will you keep on track, or get back on track, when the buzz of society enters the picture? You may want to bookmark this page in your journal because we are human and reminders are a good thing!

Mind:

Ryan loves the movie *City Slickers*. There is a scene where Mitch (Billy Crystal) and Curly (Jack Palance) are riding horses side by side. Curly is a leathery-skinned trail boss with

Day 15

a gruff voice. His presence is intimidating. As the two ride alone in the beautiful, desolate mountains, Curly gives Mitch some life advice. He asks Mitch if he knows the secret of life. As Curly asks his question, he holds his index finger in the air. Puzzled, Mitch replies, "Your finger?"

Curly explains the secret is "one thing." Nothing else matters. But Curly never tells Mitch what the "one thing" is because it's different for everyone.

And you? What is your "one thing"? What are the various roles you have in this life? For me, I am a wife, mom, sister, friend, relative, employee, athlete, fitness instructor, life coach and author. Choose one role that you'd like to focus on. Write it in your journal. What is the "one thing" that, if done consistently well, can guarantee your success?

I work for a company which is committed to improving the lives of patients with cancer. I personally represent a few medications that help with specific malignancies. My "one thing" is focusing on the patients I am affecting. When I take the time to realize that each patient is someone's son, daughter, father, mother, brother, sister or friend... when I imagine what their personal stories might be, my passion for their remissions fuels my success and my drive for excellence.

How can you remind yourself of your "one thing"? What will you do to keep this on the forefront of your mind? Can you think of "one thing" for each of your roles? Keep track of these thoughts in your journal and put them into action!

Body:

(Y)ou were bought at a price. Therefore honor God with your body. (1 Corinthians 6:20)

Assuming God is your greatest "one thing," what do you think 1 Corinthians 6:20 means when it says to honor Him with your body? Write your thoughts in your journal. In what ways are you currently honoring God with your body? How about in terms of your fitness and nutrition?

Are there ways where you feel you might not be glorifying Him? Is there "one thing" you can commit to do today which will drive all of your other behaviors and start a winning and glorious chain reaction? For me, my "one thing" is my early morning workouts. When I start my day successfully nurturing my body, it motivates me to keep on that same path. I don't want to negate my workout, so I am more focused on hydrating well and eating clean foods. What's your "one thing"? Write it out in your journal and commit to it!

Day 16

My thirty-first birthday didn't start out the way I would have expected. I grew up in a family where birthdays were a big deal. It didn't matter if one of our birthdays fell on a weekday; it didn't even matter if you had grown up and already moved out of the house. It was a known fact that we would all get together and celebrate that special person's birth*date* (not a day early and not a day late). What a fantastic tradition that was 30 years strong in my life.

I was living with my sister at the time, but the condo was empty when I woke up. Lori had already left to take care of our Mom and Dad who both had cancer. It was painfully obvious that Mom was in the very last stage of her valiant battle. For Dad, it was tough to tell which was worse: his non-Hodgkin's lymphoma or his broken heart. So I roamed around the house doing nothing in particular. Ryan was my boyfriend at that point and, being a musician... well... you can imagine a musician's hours. I didn't expect a call from him for another couple of hours.

Since I wasn't doing well with the silence, I called over to my parents' house. My Dad picked up the phone and somberly wished me a happy birthday. He took a long pause and said, "I'm so sorry. I don't think we can do anything with you today. Hopefully Ryan can take you out." Although I fully understood it would be impossible to celebrate with them, my heart sank. This was the end of a 30-year tradition. I got off the phone, laid on my bed with my dogs and cried.

A couple hours later, the phone rang and it was my first cheerful birthday call. "Hi honey! I was hoping to spend the day with you."

My spirit woke back up. "I'd love that Ryan. What should I wear?" Now, anyone with estrogen can see through my question. Yes, it was a tactical one. But it was also a very savvy way of understanding his intentions.

"Dress warm and casual." Ugh... obviously not a romantic date. No one bundles up in comfy layers for romance. Oh well, at least we were celebrating.

Although I lived 15 minutes away from the beach, he drove us inland. This was his second non-romantic move, but who's keeping score, right? We stopped for lunch at a burger joint (no, I didn't think *third* non-romantic move... well... maybe...) and then we seemed to be driving aimlessly through the town where I went to college. I will say that to know Ryan is to love him. So, in spite of my sarcasm, I actually loved every second of just being with him and all his randomness. We eventually ended up in the beautiful mountain community of Lake Arrowhead. The scene was perfectly romantic: the sky was bright blue with rolling clouds; snow was on the ground; the town was decorated for Christmas, there wasn't a detail missing; you could even hear Christmas music as a backdrop. I held Ryan's hand as we strolled.

He took me to a quaint restaurant where he had a reservation. Now, this really caught me off guard. "Ryan" and "reservation" weren't typically spoken in the same breath. After dinner, he asked if I wanted my presents. "Of course!" With a smile he handed me what was obviously a CD by its size and shape. The cynic in me was saying, "Yeah, now that was personal and thoughtful... not!" I took the ribbon and wrapping off, and I felt like time stopped. The cynic in me couldn't have missed the mark more. The words on the CD case read, "Completed With Your Love... A love song for the love of

Day 16

my life Noelle." My hands were shaking and tears welled up in my eyes as I opened the case to read the love letter inside, "...You have filled in the blank void that was deliberately put there by God... You are my Malachi blessing. I hope you enjoy listening to this song for the rest of your life because I wrote it from the bottom of my heart... I love you and Happy 31st Birthday this day, December 16, 2001."

I told Ryan I wanted to leave so we could listen in the car. He pulled out a personal CD player. "Open the companion gift first." As I did, I cried. Ryan had framed the lyrics of his song to me. I put the headphones on and could not believe the beauty... the blessings... the most intimate love I had ever experienced.

And when I think of all the ways you've made my life so much brighter
I know that God has opened the floodgates from above
And when I look into your eyes I feel a burning desire
Filling my body completely with your love

"Completed With Your Love" – Ryan Dey

Can you get the picture in your mind of a lady with tears streaming down her face... she looks beautifully radiant and the tears somehow add to her grace? Well, I looked nothing like that. I started sobbing and I was crying the ugly cry. I could feel my nose running, so I used my sleeve to wipe it, only to be mortified as I saw a line of snot connecting my nose to my sleeve. When the song was done, I looked up at Ryan. He was smiling with an open hand offering up the most beautiful diamond ring, "Noelle? Will you marry me?"

No, my thirty-first birthday didn't start out the way I would have expected. Nor did it end the way I would have expected. God put an end to one tradition in order to open the door for new possibilities.

APPLICATIONS

Heart:

To know a love this deep is to have just a tiny glimpse of God's love for us. Isn't it crazy that He loves us even more than this? So, in my life I have sought to understand this as best as I can. I want to always be in love with God through Jesus. In my attempts, I have analyzed the "Gospels" of Matthew, Mark, Luke and John—reading the words Jesus spoke. I studied His birth, life, ministry, death and resurrection. I tried to know Him better by reading and re-reading the Psalms. I spent quiet times studying the letters Paul wrote to the churches to learn from his wisdom about God. Although this learning is imperative, I found myself a bit unfulfilled, like I was reading in third person. It was a great history lesson and all, but I didn't feel connected. I wanted to be *in love*.

I now have a rich relationship with God, one that is a love story written in first person. The darn thing is, when I tried to put my finger on how I went from third person to first person, I couldn't figure it out. I ended up asking Ryan what advice he would give to help someone fall in love with God. He said, "It's experiential. I can read about the vastness of God, but I feel it in a sunset." Oh wow. I think we're onto something. We can read about the miracles of Jesus, but we experience them when we see a child being born. We can read about the tender love of God, but we feel it as we wipe away the tears from our child's eyes. Ryan further explained how

Day 16

we can learn so much about our Creator when we marvel at His creation.

In our family, we have a deep love for Lake Tahoe. Its beauty is breathtaking. The lake is majestic. The Sierra Nevadas are rugged, strong and bold. At dawn and dusk, the sky is grand beyond comprehension. Although Lake Tahoe is magnificent, it also has detailed intricacies. Funny little squirrels run around the ground, gather the peanuts we set out for them, stuff them in their cheeks and run up the trees.

Look at what that means about God's character. The words used to describe Lake Tahoe are words that point to the Creator. He is rugged, strong, bold... He cares about minute details... He is grand... He has a hysterical sense of humor. You get the picture. So, what lights your heart on fire? What can you learn about God through that? This is just a tiny glimpse of our God who is beyond comprehension.

Journal your thoughts and write a love letter to God to let Him know that you yearn to have a first person, intimate love relationship with Him. In your prayers, continue to ask God to give you an unquenchable desire for Jesus. Ask God to help you fall in love with Him. I've learned to pray for that desire and to be honest when I don't have that love in my heart. It's been my ongoing, persistent prayer. He honored my prayer and He will honor yours as well!

Mind:

There is a time for everything,
and a season for every activity under heaven:
a time to be born and a time to die,
a time to plant and a time to uproot,
a time to kill and a time to heal,

a time to tear down and a time to build,
a time to weep and a time to laugh,
a time to mourn and a time to dance (Ecclesiastes 3:1-4)

Have you been holding onto any "traditions" because you dread the mourning process of letting go? I'm not the only one who lies on the bed with dogs to cry, am I? Maybe you're in an on-again-off-again dating relationship and you know in your heart of hearts it's about comfort, not love. Or, you might be in a job that doesn't align with your values or your God-given talents. For some of us, our tradition can be as broad as a mindset or a way of living.

At one time, that "tradition" probably suited you because it was the "season" for it. But, there's also a season to have it die... a time when we need to weep and mourn over what used to be. Without that, we cannot bring in the new season of healing, dancing and laughing. In your journal, write down the old traditions you need to uproot so God can make room for your new season. Also, write what your new season will look like: what will your new traditions be? Get excited. Dancing and laughing are straight ahead!

Body:

We can knowingly or unknowingly create "traditions" with our health and wellness. One of my friends told me that she marked the end of every day with a glass of wine. The wine signified a job well done and she associated it with comfort and relaxation. But then she realized that her old tradition didn't fit in with her new tradition of waking up early for her 5:30

Day 16

a.m. boot camp class. Although it wasn't easy to let that tradition fall by the wayside, she found different ways to signify comfort and relaxation in the form of bubble baths complete with a glass of spa-inspired iced water with lemon slices.

Another friend of mine had the habit of snacking when stressed. He thought the snacking was helping him manage his stress until he stepped on the scale. Now you can find him taking a brisk walk in the fresh air. It conquers the same goal with better outcomes.

Here are other "traditions" that I just love (sarcasm from a fitness instructor): females who don't lift weights; people who read while on a piece of cardio equipment (if you are able to read, you're not working hard enough... get your iPod on and work!); those people who "don't have time" for exercise; fast food junkies who say they're too busy to eat well... Oh, don't get me going. Challenge your traditions. Come up with creative solutions; write them in your journal and in your calendar. If you don't have a solution (Really? Even after praying about it? Even after Googling your question?), hop on a discussion board such as www.sparkpeople.com and ask those who have had success in areas where you struggle. Journal your plan. Well? Get moving!

Day 17

When I initially started writing this morning, I began this paragraph by saying, "Our family, like every family has one side with a handful of nuts... those relatives who have a few screws loose." But looking at those words, I realize that if I'm being honest, our family actually has *both* sides filled with nuts and loose screws. If I take it even one step further, I realize my husband and I are probably the biggest offenders of that statement. I guess we should start calling our daughter "Peanut."

If you saw my side of the family, by appearance alone you'd probably guess that we are all mild-mannered and conservative. You might assume we laugh the stereotypical Japanese giggle as we demurely cover our mouths. I don't want to burst your bubble, but... POP!

At our big annual New Year's Day gatherings at my great-aunt and uncle's house, there is loud conversation, hysterical laughter and sarcastic humor. And, in addition to enjoying each other's company, the highlight of the celebration is, by far, the food. There's homemade traditional Japanese food that looks as beautiful as artwork and there's the American fare complete with fried chicken and homemade potato salad. Every coffee table has a beautiful Oriental bowl filled with senbei (Japanese rice crackers). The mixture of those crackers varies in shapes and sizes. Some mixes also include dried peas. For whatever reason, most of us "kids" grew up loving senbei, minus the dehydrated peas.

With that being said, Lori got the great idea to play a practical joke on one of our cousins. Lori carefully picked out every pea from the bowls and sneakily put it into our cousin's purse. We were laughing the kind of laugh that makes your sides ache, and literally silences your voice. Although our mouths were open wide and tears were streaming down our cheeks, no sounds came out. It took every amount of discipline to wait for Lisa to uncover the peas in her purse. In our imaginations, we started to play out possible scenarios. Would she find them at work while standing next to a coworker? Wouldn't it be great if she was on a date, reached for her wallet and the peas spilled out onto the ground?

We expected to get a phone call within a day or two and we couldn't wait to hear how it all unfolded. Well, after the days turned into a week, and the week turned into a month, we started to question ourselves. Could she possibly have been offended? Did she think *she* put the peas in her purse? Wouldn't it be horrible if she gave someone else the credit for the brilliant joke? Lori eventually broke down and called her, although it seemed to take away from the genius of the situation.

"Weeelllll?" Lori inquired.

"Well what?" Lisa replied.

"The peas!"

"What peas?"

I listened to my sister's side of the conversation as she relived each detail. Then Lori replied with something that sounded like this, "No, your *black* purse. The one with the short strap and the pockets on the side." Uh-oh. We could see exactly where this was heading. To our dismay, the pea-infused purse belonged to our auntie's elderly mom: the one who actually *is* quiet and demure, standing well under five feet tall; the one who is pure sweetness, with no ounce of sarcasm; the one who rarely talks, but when she does, you have to stretch your ears to hear her; the only one you'd never want to play a practical joke on. Oops.

Day 17

APPLICATIONS

Heart:

I can still feel the emotions we went through waiting... anticipating the laughter and joy from our cousin. I still remember how I couldn't wait for her to give us the due honor and credit for being so creative and making her day.

It then made me wonder if God ever has those same pained emotions... eagerly waiting for me to thank Him for His wonderfully unique and creative gifts which He showers on my life. I wonder how many gifts I've missed because I wasn't seeking them out. Now, I don't let myself feel guilty for past misses. I recognize where I fell short, pray for forgiveness and receive His restoration. But, that thought challenges me to expect that God, who loves me to extents I cannot comprehend, is blessing me abundantly moment by moment and I don't want to miss a single gift.

Now on his way to Jerusalem, Jesus traveled along the border between Samaria and Galilee. As he was going into a village, ten men who had leprosy met him. They stood at a distance and called out in a loud voice, "Jesus, Master, have pity on us!"

When he saw them, he said, "Go, show yourselves to the priests." And as they went, they were cleansed.

One of them, when he saw he was healed, came back, praising God in a loud voice. He threw himself at Jesus' feet and thanked him—and he was a Samaritan.

Jesus asked, "Were not all ten cleansed? Where are the other nine? Was no one found to return and give praise to God except this foreigner?" Then he said to him, "Rise and go; your faith has made you well." (Luke 17:11-19)

I believe all ten of the lepers must have been ecstatic and grateful for their gift of healing. But I do find it interesting that even though all of them cried out to Jesus in their misery, 90 percent of them neglected to praise Him and give Him gratitude when they received His miraculous gift... His perfect answer to their cry. If I'm honest with myself, I can say that there have been many times when I've dropped to my knees to bring my heartfelt, gut-wrenching prayers to God and when He answered my prayers, I was quick to share the good news with my family and friends before I shared my joy and thankfulness to the Giver and Author of those incomparable gifts.

Do you have any answered prayers where you neglected to give praise to God? Devote several pages in your journal (or have a separate journal) specifically for gratitude. Start your list! List out the gifts He has given you. Aren't you amazed at how much you've been given? Revisit this list often to see the ongoing, unbelievable blessings in your life.

Mind:

After Jesus gave the gift of healing to all ten lepers, isn't it interesting that the one who praised Jesus in a loud voice and threw himself at Jesus' feet was a foreigner? Where were all the Jews? I mean if anyone should have been quick to thank Jesus, wouldn't it have been those who were considered to be His people?

Day 17

Why is it so easy to take the people we love the most—those who are closest to us—for granted? It hit me like a brick upside my head one morning when I realized the amount of grace and understanding I give my friends and acquaintances was actually greater than what I give my own family.

These are the same people I begged God to bring to my life. In my grandest dreams, I never could have imagined a husband as awesome as Ryan. And together, we received a gift unimaginable in our daughter Sierra. The first time we saw her picture, we broke down in tears of joy and overwhelm.

Make a list of the people who are closest to you in your journal. Were there special things you did for them when the relationship was new that you haven't done in a while? Write out those actions. Circle an action from that list that you can do for them today. How can you ensure that they get the best of you? Make a commitment to treat them the same way you did when you first fell in love with them.

Body:

What are your physical gifts? If you have a stocky build, you are created with more fast-twitch fibers that are geared for speed and explosive strength. Those with lanky physiques are dominated by slow-twitch fibers and tend to have natural endurance. For the longest time, I obsessed over what I didn't have and what I couldn't do. Why couldn't I run long distances like my friend whose legs are longer than my whole body? Then, comedy arose when I heard her frustration since she couldn't sprint faster than me.

Certainly we can work on our weaknesses, but we should define ourselves by our God-authored gifts. Physically, what comes naturally to you? Do you have endurance? Strength? Do you have powerful legs? Are your arms muscular? When you exercise today, focus solely on your God-given gifts, and give thanks as you do.

What about your nutritional gifts? I live in Southern California, so there are affordable health food stores and weekly farmers markets within a quick drive. Maybe you live somewhere where you can grow your own produce. Are you a talented cook who can recreate some family favorite recipes to be healthier yet still yummy? Do you have a group of friends who would want to gather on a weekly or monthly basis? I've heard of groups where each person makes a huge batch of their favorite healthy meal and they prepackage one for each of their friends. So everyone leaves with a variety of healthy homemade meals that are set for the freezer until it's time to reheat and feed the family in a matter of minutes. We all have gifts… what are yours? How can you implement them? Are you thanking God for them? Journal your thoughts. Praise God for your gifts!

Day 18

My sister Lori gave me a heartfelt compliment recently. I was having one of those days where I could literally feel the grey hairs sprouting out of my head and I was naming each of them after my daughter. I was furious with some of Sierra's choices so I put her on a timeout. But, when her sentence was over, I showed my forgiveness by giving her a big hug and I acted silly to break the tension. The sweet words from my sister were, "Oh Noey, I am so excited you have broken through our family's cycle. Sierra marks our first generation which will know grace and forgiveness." Now, I happen to be someone who loves praise and readily accepts it, however this time, it wasn't mine to own.

Yes, the heaviness of grudge-holding and relentless anger had been broken, but it wasn't changed in Sierra's generation, it was changed in *my* generation. Unmerited grace wasn't regularly given to my sister and me as we grew up. Our Mom and Dad were amazing people who genuinely loved us, but I can count on three fingers the amount of times my Mom apologized to me. And one of those times, the apology was yelled, "Well, if that's what you think Noelle Kelly Sase, then I AM SORRY!" Our family's vicious cycle was actually broken by my big sister and I was the main recipient.

I am six years younger than Lori and for most of our lives I was the typical kid sis. Lori desperately wanted to play soccer when she was little. My parents said "No!" for years before they finally let her play. I couldn't care less about sports, but I was on a soccer *and* basketball team by the time I was six. When her friends came over, our Mom would say, "Let Noelle play too." I was bossy. I lied and Lori would be the one to get in trouble. I wasn't half the student my sister was. In fact, my Mom got to know the vice principal extremely well when I was in high school due to my antics (if I explained what I meant by *antics*, you might faint).

And then there was Lori... she has always been humble, honest and she was a magna cum laude student. So, you can easily guess who got the accolades in our family, right? Correct-a-mundo if you said me. What?! I know, I know... if you were in her shoes, you'd probably call a hit man, eh? Well then, I'm glad I didn't have you as my sibling.

Don't get me wrong, it's not like I didn't get in trouble. I gave our parents high highs and very low lows. In addition to the accolades, I also got kicked out of our house and I was told, "You'll never amount to anything." There were a few times when my Mom told me she disowned me as her daughter. My Mom had a wonderfully warm personality, unless you offended her. In many of those cases, you had a permanent black mark against you. When that happened to me, I told her I didn't care what she thought and that I could make it on my own. But truthfully speaking, I did care. I wanted to be loved. I wanted someone to believe in me. I wanted a do-over. God knew my truest heart's cry and generously responded by giving me Lori as a sister.

Against all odds, Lori became a Christian at a young age. She was the only one in our family who had the Holy Spirit beaming through her. When she first told our Mom about her relationship with the Lord, she was commanded to "not speak the name of God in our house." Lori has faced the most horrific spiritual attacks from the time she was a kid. If I were in her shoes, I'm not sure I would have remained so committed... so deeply in love with Jesus... but she has never wavered. And because of that, she has also never given up on

Day 18

anyone... especially me... because she knows that God can and will move mountains. I am convinced that one of the main reasons our parents and I became Christians was Lori's unwavering heart.

She was in college when I got kicked out of the house. There weren't cell phones back then, and I didn't have enough money to call her from pay phones. So Lori devised a plan where I would call her collect from a specific phone where she knew the call back number. If I used my real name, she'd accept the charges knowing it was extremely urgent. If I gave a fake name to the operator, Lori would decline the collect call and call me right back. We still crack up when we think back to the day when I used a heavy unspecified accent and told the operator my name was "Racchhmahn."

When most everyone discarded me as being "one of *those* kids," I always had Lori's gentle voice tell me, "You're amazing. Not only are you athletic—you're smart, beautiful and you make me laugh. I love you so much." Lori healed me through affirmation, and by her grace she allowed me the freedom to wipe the slate clean and to grow into the woman that God created me to be.

APPLICATIONS

Heart:

Do you remember back when we studied the story of the prodigal son in Luke 15:11-32? It was so freeing to realize that no matter how ugly our past, God throws a party when we come back to Him! That story has been one of my life's greatest themes. But the part of the story we didn't look at was the viewpoint of the brother who honored and obeyed his father his entire life. He never had a party thrown for him.

Transformation by Truth

He was rightfully angry and didn't want to join in the festivities that were being thrown for his brother who disrespected his dad on many levels including throwing his money away on prostitutes. Here's how his dad responded:

"'My son,' the father said, 'you are always with me, and everything I have is yours. But we had to celebrate and be glad, because this brother of yours was dead and is alive again; he was lost and is found.'" (Luke 15:31-32)

Have you ever found yourself in a similar situation? What if you're the one in your marriage who is reading self-help books and putting in all of the effort, but your spouse takes no notice? At your job, you are honest and highly qualified but someone with questionable work ethic and less experience gets the promotion. Maybe you're taking the high road by not speaking poorly about your ex-spouse and now your kids are siding against you. Have you ever thought, "It's just not worth the effort. I'm getting nowhere!" How can you find peace in the dad's response in the story of the prodigal son? How does it affect you to know that God is taking notice of you and that all He has is yours? What would your world look like if you treated that response as being 100 percent true? Journal your responses to your specific situations.

Galatians 6:9 says it this way, *"Let us not become weary in doing good, for at the proper time we will reap a harvest if we do not give up."* My sister had to wait a few decades (and then some) to reap her full harvest with me. Words cannot begin to describe my gratitude since she didn't grow weary while doing good. What can you do to remind yourself that you are *promised* your harvest if you don't become weary and lose

Day 18

heart? Place your answer somewhere where you will see it often.

Mind:

Hanging onto resentment is letting someone you despise live rent-free in your head. —Ann Landers

I've gone to enough counseling appointments and I've read enough books to know that forgiveness is at least as important, if not *more* important, for the one forgiving rather than the recipient. To give undeserved grace doesn't mean that you're saying the offense afflicted on you was justified. But, consider the freedom you will have if you break the heavy bond that is linking you to someone who hurt you.

I had to go through these exercises after my parents had died. It was eye opening to me when I was asked, "Have you noticed that your Mom is still controlling you and she's not even here anymore?" Can you think of situations where you need to give eviction notices to the tenants living rent-free in your head? What actions will you take this very moment to release yourself and the tenants? Journal your answer and get on it... now!

Body:

Any chance you're tired of doing all the "right things" when it comes to your health and fitness? I had a client tell me the other day that it just wasn't fair that she was the only one in her group of family and friends who made the healthy choices at restaurants, journaled her food and stayed committed to an exercise program. I asked her what her goals were. They were to lose weight, be a healthy role model for her kids and to increase her energy.

When she got herself away from judging what was "fair" and "unfair" and got back to focusing on what her story was, the fog cleared and she was back on track. Do you need to put your blinders on and refocus on the healthy life God is calling you to? List the benefits of staying on track in your journal, even when things seem unfair. So then, what is on your schedule today for healthy living? Schedule it in with a permanent pen and do it without growing weary. Your harvest is waiting!

Day 19

When my Mom got her initial cancer diagnosis, the statistics said she would live somewhere between nine months to a year. By God's loving grace and by the brilliance of Dr. Barth, she survived her battle six-and-a-half years. I remember people telling me back then, "You should be so grateful you had your Mom for so long!" Were they right? Yes. Well, kind of.

Although she and I had our differences, this was my *Mom*... the one who was supposed to be the first to greet us in the airport when we brought Sierra home from China... the lady who would have found immense joy in her granddaughter and would have baked her homemade chocolate chip cookies... the grandma who would have spoiled Sierra with gifts and so many sweets I'd roll my eyes in disbelief ... she was the one Lori and I wanted to do ladies' lunches with and as always, each of us would fight to pay the bill.

The skies were grey and it was raining on the morning of her funeral. It seemed symbolic because I was in my own storm. A week ago my Mom had died. I was getting married in just over a month. My Dad was losing his battle to non-Hodgkin's Lymphoma. Although at the time, we had no idea that he would only be separated from his bride for a mere 62 days.

My quiet time seemed to be as dark and solemn as the skies. I couldn't hear God through the numbness in my mind. I didn't know how to reach for His hand. So instead I put my workout clothes on and headed for the gym. Once I got there I realized I forgot my iPod. To me, this is the kiss of death when I'm running on a treadmill. *"W-h-a-t-e-v-e-r*!

Transformation by Truth

Is there anything else that could make this day worse, God?" My frustration with God fueled my run. I was on a treadmill which faced a huge window. I watched the rolling clouds as techno music pounded through my body.

And then... in the most unlikely setting... God healed my heart. Smack dab in the middle of heavy, threatening clouds, three brilliant rays of light shone through, piercing the darkness. The obnoxious booming music faded into the next song which was "I Hope You Dance," written by Tia Sillers and Mark Sanders, sung by Lee Ann Womak. It was truly the last song that you'd ever hear in a gym. As I listened closely to the lyrics, I heard the wisdom that both my tender, loving Lord and my deeply missed Mom would have whispered in my ear:

I hope you never lose your sense of wonder
You get your fill to eat
But always keep that hunger
May you never take one single breath for granted
God forbid love ever leave you empty handed
I hope you still feel small
When you stand beside the ocean
Whenever one door closes, I hope one more opens
Promise me you'll give faith a fighting chance

And when you get the choice to sit it out or dance
I hope you dance

I hope you never fear those mountains in the distance
Never settle for the path of least resistance
Living might mean taking chances
But they're worth taking
Loving might be a mistake

Day 19

> *But it's worth making*
> *Don't let some hell bent heart*
> *Leave you bitter*
> *When you come close to selling out*
> *Reconsider*
> *Give the heavens above*
> *More than just a passing glance*
>
> *And when you get the choice to sit it out or dance*
> *I hope you dance*

I'm not one who has ever audibly heard God's voice, nor has He ever communicated with me through visions. But at that most precious, intimate moment, I had a picture in my mind of my Mom with her arms stretched out, her eyes facing toward the sun, twirling in circles dancing. It was the perfect visual because at every party, she was the first one on the dance floor. And by the way, you would have been the second because she would have inevitably grabbed your hand and led you to the dance floor whether she knew you or not. The magnitude of her restoration was wonderfully healing. The last time I saw her, her tiny body must've only weighed about 75 pounds. She had been sick for what felt like ages. But now, she is complete! She is dancing! I will never stop replaying that scene in my mind until I reunite with her in heaven.

APPLICATIONS

Heart:

> *I pray also that the eyes of your heart may be enlightened in order that you may know the hope to which he has called you, the riches*

of his glorious inheritance in the saints, and his incomparably great power for us who believe. That power is like the working of his mighty strength, which he exerted in Christ when he raised him from the dead and seated him at his right hand in the heavenly realms, far above all rule and authority, power and dominion, and every title that can be given, not only in the present age but also in the one to come. (Ephesians 1:18-21)

My heart leaps when I read, "the eyes of your heart." What does this mean to you? Paul addresses those of us who believe. Look at the sequence of events that occur when the eyes of our hearts are enlightened: we will have the knowledge of hope, an understanding of riches which are our inheritance and we will comprehend the incomparably great power that we have living in us. And... it's not reserved for heaven, after our time on earth is over... but it's also for the "present age." We are talking about the same power that raised Jesus from the dead. We can have all of this now!

During the last months before my Mom died, "the eyes of my heart" were heavy. They held visions of her failing body writhed in pain. Although I knew of the reality of heaven... at least, I tried to grasp the concept occasionally... the visions of my scrawny, frail, jaundiced Mom plagued my soul. It wasn't until that life-changing morning of her funeral when I began to let God enlighten the eyes of my heart. By faith, I removed the visions of her that haunted me and I replaced them with the perfect illustration of her twirling and dancing. The old visuals I held onto were what her life used to be. They were past-tense. The here and now is completely different. I began my journey of seeing with the eyes of my heart guided by God's truths. My Mom is dancing!

Day 19

In your journal, write your own reflections. What do the "eyes of your heart" see? Do you have any damaging visuals in your heart? Inevitably your life has been scarred with your own heartache. What do your deepest pains look like? How can you let God enlighten those destructive pictures? What do God's inspired, truth-filled images look like? Ask God in prayer what the hope is that He is calling you to. What are the riches He is giving to you by His glorious inheritance? How can you harness His incomparably great power and live this life which will continue through eternity? Take the time, not just this moment—but from here on, to carefully seek His answers. Each time you uncover another piece of your unique puzzle, add it to your journal.

Mind:

There was a time when I was challenged to approach my life's goals as if I were writing a screenplay. This concept encouraged me to visualize the story I desired. Once I saw it in my mind, I was able to play my role and live the adventure. How can you apply this to your life?

I used to take a boot camp class at the gym. I loved how the exercises were based on basic athletic drills since I stick out like a sore thumb in the classes that have any amount of choreography. Unfortunately the instructor quit and the class got cancelled. I used to complain to Ryan each time I'd come home from the gym after another subpar workout. He told me that I should become an instructor and teach the class myself. I tried to explain how I was nothing like the instructors at the gym. I had no musicality and I didn't have the right look. Ryan continued to encourage me, telling me that I could do it.

After a while, I started to believe him. So I began to daydream. I pictured myself coaching my own boot camp class. In my mind, I could see the drills. I pictured the athletes doing their push-ups. I could see them running sprint drills. But I also wanted to integrate life coaching and motivational speaking. I created a unique story which I hadn't seen in any other fitness class. Once I wrote that script in my mind, I took the steps needed so I could play my role. I earned my certifications to be a group fitness instructor and a professional life coach. I got experience by teaching at a large gym chain. From there, I partnered with the city where I live and created my own boot camp company.

Write down one goal that you want to focus on now. Use your imagination to create your story. Who else will be co-starring in your play? Think about how it feels emotionally. What do you look like physically? Does your day-to-day life look different than it is now? See your play in fine detail.

After you write your screenplay, it will be time to engineer it into reality. What resources do you need? Have you read books on the subject? Should you use Google to seek out practical instructions? Do you know someone who has had success that you can contact for advice? Write your story and enjoy every second of playing your part!

Body:

My Dad was ahead of his time. That was the good news. The bad news: I had no idea how amazing he was. Before I was ten years old, he used to make me shoot free throws in my mind. While my teammates would goof around on the basketball courts, my Dad would tell me, "Shoot 100 in your mind. Watch the ball swoosh through the net. If it nicks

Day 19

the rim, start again. Nothing but net." Sometimes I'd do it. Other times I would close my eyes and wonder when I could turn the Atari on again (think Xbox 360 with none of the cool capabilities). I was a pretty good free throw shooter. And that was using about 50 percent of my potential!

Now that I am a coach, what do I tell my clients? Visualize, visualize, visualize! When they can picture themselves with their end results... down to every detail of muscle definition... when they can watch themselves in their minds doing an exercise like they are watching a movie and they are in the starring role, I can literally see them move faster and with more power. The thing is, our bodies react similarly whether the experiences we have are in our minds or if they are actually happening.

In your workouts, play your own movie in your mind. See yourself doing your exercises successfully. Picture yourself with the muscle definition you desire. Feel the emotional momentum as well. That starts the snowball effect. When using these techniques, you'll move faster and exert more power physically. That will result in more calories burned and you will create stronger, leaner muscles. That will lead to increased self-confidence. Confidence begets success.

What would your fitness and nutrition look like if we were watching a movie called, "A Day in the Life of the Unstoppable Athlete (Enter Your Name)"? Before you gear up for your workout and before you eat clean today, write that desired vision in your journal and see it in your mind's eyes. Don't miss a single detail. Now go tackle your workout and nourish your body well!

Day 20

I grew up in a very budget-conscious family. My Mom was a brilliant homemaker. She cut coupons, mapped out what was on sale at each market and by the time she finished her weekly shopping, the markets owed her money (no exaggeration). As a kid, I'll admit I didn't really appreciate her thriftiness, and here's why: when it was popular to wear the Dolfins nylon running shorts that Richard Simmons made famous, mine were Dolphins (notice the "ph" in my Dolphins as opposed to the "f" in the name brand Dolfins); when the cool kids wore Polo shirts, my golf-style shirt had a man on a horse without a polo stick; and my Adidas-like shoes had four stripes.

Early in their marriage, my parents bought their dream home, which was "way out in the boondocks" as far as friends and family were concerned. Dad scraped all the money he had to barely afford the payments on their 27,000 dollar home. The "boondocks" community grew through the years, well-to-do families moved in and it eventually became known as an upper-middle class, highly sought after neighborhood. I attended University High School in Irvine and many of my classmates were receiving really nice cars on their sixteenth birthdays. I asked my Dad if I could have a car of my own when I turned 16. He said, "Sure. Just make sure you pay cash in full... absolutely no car payments." Hmm, not necessarily the answer I was hoping for.

I worked part-time jobs and recycled newspapers and cans. Eventually when I was 18, I became the proud owner of a beaten down '67 Mustang with no power steering, no power brakes, no power clutch, no air conditioning and no radio. The paint had a "matte finish" which was a fancy way to say, "There ain't no way to get this baby to shine!" As I drove, my muscles would literally shake with all of the brake and clutch pushing. Oh yeah... I almost forgot... I took the widest turns you've ever seen. Pedestrians beware!

After I graduated college and got my first "real" job as a copier sales representative, my Dad said, "Maybe it's time you get a more reliable car." After multiple trips to car lots with my Dad, I ended up with a brand new, base-model pick-up truck. Man, was it shiny and gorgeous! I still didn't have a radio or air conditioning, but it drove like a dream *with* power steering, power brakes and a power clutch.

I had the truck for about a year when I drove my manager to accompany me on a sales call. He was a big guy, although only average in height. When he got in, his knees jammed against the glove compartment because I had to have the bench seat forward enough so I could reach the pedals. Five minutes into our drive, I noticed he was sweating.

"Hey Noelle, put on the air."

"You'll have to roll your window down. I don't have A/C."

"Well, can you at least turn on the radio?"

"Your voice *is* the radio... start singing if you want music!"

When we arrived at the account, his expensive dress shirt was sticking to his back with sweat. So can you imagine my elation two years later when I bought my little green Saturn? It not only had power steering, power brakes, a power clutch, but it also had working air conditioning, an AM/FM radio and a cassette player! I was such a proud owner. Now looking back, I am overflowing with gratitude that I didn't get a car

Day 20

parked in the garage for my sixteenth birthday. There is no way I would have appreciated the gift to the extent I should have. I also would have been robbed of monumental life lessons and the true joy that came from hard work and patience. It nearly brings me to tears remembering my Dad and Mom asking for a test ride. My Dad was in the passenger seat, and my Mom crawled into back. Both of them had a silent smile filled with pride as we drove with no destination in mind... all three of us were just enjoying the ride.

APPLICATIONS

Heart:

Did my parents have the ability to buy a nice car for me when I first got my license? Well, not a luxury car... they couldn't afford that for themselves. But, I imagine they could have bought me the pick-up truck. With my limited know-it-all teenage mindset, that decision made perfect sense. I mean they loved me and all, right? Well... actually, the wisdom in my parents' decision was greater than what I could comprehend at that time. They allowed me to learn how to take care of, and have pride in what I *did* have. I also received a first-hand lesson in the satisfaction of delayed gratification. With that, the true gifts they lavished on me were far superior to a new car. They gave me the opportunity to build determination, patience and integrity.

(W)e also rejoice in our sufferings, because we know that suffering produces perseverance; perseverance, character; and character, hope. And hope does not disappoint us... (Romans 5:3-5)

Are you getting tired of taking the "high road" with little results? What is your situation? Journal your current struggle. It's okay to be detailed in your frustrations. Many of us assume we have to clean up our prayers to make them acceptable to God. Isn't that comical? As if God doesn't already know! David was so real with his emotions—good and bad—in the Psalms he wrote. At the same time, he always brought his focus back to praising God. In Acts 13:22, God calls David a *"man after my own heart."*

So, aiming to follow David's lead, re-read Romans 5:3-5 and explain in your journal how perseverance, hope and character are being woven into your moral and spiritual fibers. Although these might not be classified as the happiest times in your life, wouldn't you agree that it is possible to rejoice due to your character being built up and gaining the hope that doesn't disappoint?

Mind:

How are you loving, appreciating and nurturing what you *do* have? There are so many times in my life when I miss the gift of my current blessings because I'm too busy drooling over what might be ahead.

Sierra's homework causes a fair amount of tension in our home. Sadly, Ryan and I don't always understand it. We'll debate (some would say "fight" but I like the way "debate" sounds) on how do it "right" while Sierra has her arms crossed, pouting and whining because we won't let her leave until everything is complete. I find myself wishing the school year could fast forward to summer vacation. Then God lovingly reminds me that I am living the dream *now* with Ryan and Sierra. There will be a day when there's no more homework.

Day 20

A time will come when she's self-sufficient and she won't be crying over non-issues (really?). Once this reality penetrated my mind and heart, I literally lost all the yearning for what might lie ahead. Thank God for these beautifully nostalgic days we have now!

You and I need to strive to hear the words, *"Well done, good and faithful servant! You have been faithful with a few things; I will put you in charge of many things. Come and share your master's happiness!" (Matthew 25:23)* Ryan and my nine-year-old Sierra are the "few things" that I am called to be faithful with. This is my calling now. If God puts me "in charge of many things" in the future, that will be my calling at that appointed time.

What mind shift can you make today to be a "good and faithful servant"? What are the "few things" that you need to be faithful with? How can you stop yearning for what you don't have and take care of what you do have? Journal your thoughts.

Body:

If there was a miracle pill that would give you the perfect body, would you take it? The diet industry is a multi-billion dollar industry. Did you catch that? Multi. Billion. Well, how is it working? You know the facts… It's not! If you were given what you view as a perfect body, would you know how to maintain it? Thinking of it in another way, if you gave a chain smoker a new set of lungs, would that smoker keep the new lungs healthy and clean?

Getting healthier is a journey. It's not a quick pit stop. But, here's the greatest news to celebrate now: through your journey, you will love every moment of your physical transformation. You'll also be able to maintain your end results because you'll find out what works and what doesn't through your experiences. You will lose pounds, but you will gain perseverance, character and hope. You couldn't achieve those gifts with a miracle pill.

Instead of dreading your workout and your healthy habits today, visualize yourself chiseling your body and your character. Journal the joy of creating the new you. If you are currently the beaten down Mustang, know that you are well on your way to becoming the Saturn and you'll eventually be a Lamborghini! Your transformation will feel amazing… so stop focusing on the future… take the time to enjoy these roads you are traveling now!

Day 21

I can still feel my emotions remembering back to a day when I was grocery shopping and found 20 Top Ramens for a dollar. There was also a nostalgic Saturday morning when I asked the swap meet attendant how much he was asking for a pair of perfectly worn-in, authentic 501 jeans, and he answered, "Three dollars."

But, my favorite bargain that still makes me smile and laugh out loud was the leave-in conditioner I found at Pic-n-Save, which has since become Big Lots. I was a college student, so you can probably guess what my budget looked like. The year was 1993, and I was very hip with my long, permed hair (yes, it *is* natural for Japanese girls to have very large, very curly hair). The overload of chemicals took their toll, so the ends of my hair were parched. Instead of cutting my hair shorter, I set out to find a conditioner that I could leave in my hair when I wore it in a ponytail. Healthy hair was so overrated compared to length at the time.

As I strolled down the shampoo aisle, I looked closely at each bottle of conditioner that made claims to add moisture and shine. I had it narrowed down to three choices; all were priced at $1.99. However, one bottle kept *speaking* to me, "Moist and Sheen." Well, it clearly would accomplish both of my criteria: adding moisture and shine to my hair. How could I go wrong? I used it daily for 30 days. After getting out of the shower, I put the thick, almost tacky lotion through my hair. I'd pull my ponytail through the back of my baseball cap, dress in my typical white t-shirt and 501 jeans and be out the door. The smell was a little overpowering, but that was a small price to pay for the claims of Moist and Sheen.

Over the weekend, I drove back home to visit my parents. As I walked through the door and hugged my Mom, her face contorted and she quickly asked me why my hair smelled so funny. Maybe it was my insecurity, but my feelings were hurt, so I chose to keep her in the dark regarding my Pic-n-Save find. I walked away looking for my Dad. The moment I turned from my Mom, she shrieked.

"Noelle! What is wrong with your back?!"
"What are you talking about?" I fired back.
"Look!"

She grabbed me by my elbow, took me to the nearest bathroom and had me using two mirrors to clearly see the back of my shirt. There was a huge circular stain. As we systematically tried to find the cause, I hesitantly told her about the bottle of Moist and Sheen. I got it out of my overnight bag so she could see.

After long minutes of hysterical laughter (not from me, I maintained my pride), my Mom finally was able to speak clearly and informed me that I bought a generic version of Afro-Sheen. Greeaat. I must have been the first Asian to ever buy a bottle of Afro-Sheen. After telling my roommates about my dilemma, they said, "Yeah, we thought it was weird that you had that really bad sweat stain on your back all the time!"

Back in those days, it was a mystery to my parents if I'd ever graduate from college. Hmm... I wonder why they would have ever questioned my intelligence. Looking back on that illustration, I wish that I had the wit to tell my parents the "moral of the story." I could have explained that buying Moist and Sheen was a perfect example to show how

Day 21

much I valued my education. I obviously didn't put my financial resources into my three-dollar jeans or my five-cent Top Ramen. I certainly didn't use too much mental power in maintaining my afro. Instead I must have put my whole heart, all of my mind's resources, every ounce of my attention and my entire budget into my education. It wasn't the truth, but it would have given me a perfect defense for our ongoing debates!

APPLICATIONS

Heart:

The moral of that story continues to come to my mind now that I'm grown and have a family of my own. We live in a society that makes it incredibly difficult to align our hearts' resources, our minds' attention span and our finances with God's will. Buzzing cell phones, overloaded email inboxes, kids' homework and extra-curricular activities flood our to-do lists.

Even church activities can be centered around so many tasks that we forget *why* we are doing what we are doing. We come home exhausted and snap at our family members, completely forgetting that they are God's most precious gifts. Instead we choose to wear busyness like a medal of honor and forge ahead. I'm getting exhausted just thinking about this! Deep breath in, deep breath out. Let's refocus and prioritize our values to line up with the way we invest ourselves.

Be very careful, then, how you live—not as unwise but as wise, making the most of every opportunity, because the days are evil. Therefore do not be foolish, but understand what the Lord's will is. (Ephesians 5:15-17)

"(U)nderstand what the Lord's will is." Does that intimidate you? I mean how in the world are we supposed to understand what God's will is? We have a hard enough time trying to figure out what to eat for dinner. Well, let's go back to your values. List yours in order of priority (i.e.: God, my heart, spouse, children, job, Japanese afro maintenance, etc.) in your journal. Where did your relationship with God rank? Most of us will give Him top priority but neglect to dedicate time to connect with Him.

Open up your check book or your credit card statement. This is another powerful way to quantify our heart's treasures. Do your finances parallel your values? This exercise really hit me where it counted. I had to get real and dig in deep. If it is your personal mission to have God first in your life, how are you reinvesting His money?

Make adjustments, if need be, to your calendar and checkbook. "Pen in" your appointments with God. It's not that God is someone on your to-do list and once you check off that appointment, you're "done." He should be integrated in every moment of your day.

Think about this: if you were meeting with the CEO of your company, would you break the appointment because of a random errand? Well… helloooooo… this is God we are talking about! This time is far more significant and it's based on crazy amounts of love! If you break those appointments, you will miss His secret whispers and you will inevitably default to a spiral of busyness. However, if you give Him first priority, you'll gain an understanding of His desires and you'll be living a God-centered day. Even small tasks such as going to the dry

Day 21

cleaners will be purpose-filled. You will bless the people you interact with instead of just going through the motions.

As for the checkbook, God does not need your money but He does long for acts of intimacy on your part which say, "Lord, this is my heartfelt gift to you. I love you so much!" Do you need to regroup a bit or are you on target? Journal your plan.

Mind:

Now let's look at the rest of your day's schedule. One way to measure what is on your mind is to look at what consumes your day. Is your time being spent on what you value most, or have you got yourself caught in society's web of busyness? Remember, we were warned by the Apostle Paul, "Be very careful, then, how you live—not as unwise but as wise, making the most of every opportunity..." What are you doing outside of work or school during your flexible time?

Get into the habit of writing your day's goals—either first thing in the morning or the night before. That way, you can focus your mind's attention on what is most important. If your priorities are off, you will miss out on opportunities that may never come again. Write your plan in your calendar. The old adage remains, "Failing to plan is planning to fail." Let's turn that one on its head and say, "Succeeding in planning is planning to succeed!"

Body:

Getting in touch with your true self must be your first priority. —Tom Hopkins

So many of us put everyone and everything above ourselves. We think it's valiant… a trait to be admired. But truth be told, we are missing the mark living by that fallacy. My good friend and counselor likens it to a bank account. He explained that every time I am giving of myself, I am making withdrawals from my ATM. We all know that we cannot withdraw funds which don't exist, so we need to make deposits.

You scheduled in your quiet times, and those precious moments with God are deposits. Now, how are you going to take care of your body? Does your calendar reflect your workouts, clean eating, healthy meal planning and grocery market trips? What about active, fun times such as dancing, playing with kids, running around and being silly? Are you dedicating time to relax, so you can enjoy life's simple pleasures? How are you spoiling yourself? Keep in mind that your spoilings need to be in line with your physical fitness goals. Your treats might be something like a walk on the beach, a massage or a bubble bath. The best way to take care of others is to be at your personal best. That requires making deposits into your bank account. Journal your strategy and make sure your calendar reflects your plan.

The moral of *your* story now shows that you are placing your resources—your heart's desires, your mental focus, your physical health and your finances—in alignment with God's will for your life. How cool is that?! Hey Paul, we are making the most of every opportunity… thank you for that timeless wisdom! Now, back to me… how does my afro look?

End of Week Three:

I'm good enough, I'm smart enough, and doggone it, people like me! —Stuart Smalley

Although sources vary some, I think we can all agree that it takes somewhere between 21 and 30 days to create a new habit. You just completed your twenty-first day. So what are your new habits? This is a point in time where you will find yourself at a fork in the road. You might be riding on a high. You're psyched because you are living life with your heart on fire; your mind is an amazing weapon for truth; and your body is a beautiful reflection of your heart. Suh-weet! Remember to continue to celebrate throughout your entire journey.

But that might not be your story. What if you are closer to your goals, but you find yourself sabotaging your own hard efforts? For no good reason you'll find yourself at a drive thru ordering food that you know isn't worth the calories; you feel God calling you to an intimate date but you turn to your to-do list instead; your mind is obsessing over the uncontrollable factors in your life even though you know this thought process will get you nowhere. Why does this happen? There are so many reasons.

Let's revisit a foundational truth: we are living in a world at war. We have an enemy. He is dead set on using manipulative schemes in order to get you off course. You are designed to be a bright light for God and you are a threat to the enemy's dark world. With that, here are thoughts that the enemy can lodge in your mind:

- *You are selfish and self-consumed. Why aren't you using this time to take care of your family?*
- *If you continue to improve yourself, there will be greater expectations placed on you and you won't be strong enough to handle that.*
- *If you lose weight or break out of your family's dysfunctional ways, you will create unwanted attention from others. You won't have a security blanket to protect you.*
- *Your new ways make others feel worse about themselves. When you lose weight or mature emotionally and spiritually, it makes your friends' and family members' unhealthy ways more noticeable. You were created to be a rescuer, remember? No one should feel bad on your account. You need to "rescue" them from these feelings of inadequacy by not going beyond a certain point of weight loss, mental growth or spiritual maturity.*

Yes, these thoughts can come in. But it's your choice whether or not you'll admit the source (which is not God, and it's not you... it's the enemy). It's also your choice whether or not to make agreements with the lies. Don't fall into the trap and sabotage your own hard efforts!

Understand that, at this very moment, there is a battle waging for your heart, mind and body. You've already seen what the enemy's lies can look like. Remember that the enemy comes to steal, kill and destroy. Think about each of those words. Each one is vicious. Each has deadly intent. This is not hypothetical... this is your *life*. On the other hand, Jesus came to not only give you life, but He wants you to have it to the full.

The prophets spoke on behalf of God. Isaiah is generally said to be the greatest of the prophets. So when we read his words, we are reading God's words to us.

End of Week Three:

*The Spirit of the Sovereign LORD is on me,
because the LORD has anointed me
to preach good news to the poor.
He has sent me to bind up the brokenhearted,
to proclaim freedom for the captives
and release from darkness for the prisoners...*

*...and provide for those who grieve in Zion—
to bestow on them a crown of beauty
instead of ashes,
the oil of gladness
instead of mourning,
and a garment of praise
instead of a spirit of despair.
They will be called oaks of righteousness,
a planting of the LORD
for the display of his splendor. (Isaiah 61:1,3)*

Are you "poor" in your heart, mind or body? Do you feel brokenhearted? Is any insecurity, addiction or frustration making you feel like a captive prisoner? Would you like to trade your ashes for beauty... your mourning for gladness... your despair for praise? This is the life God intends for you. YOU are worth the efforts. YOU are worth fighting for. If you have fallen short of creating new habits, have no fear. Literally, have no fear!

*Shake off your dust;
rise up, sit enthroned, O Jerusalem.
Free yourself from the chains on your neck,
O captive Daughter of Zion. (Isaiah 52:2)*

Transformation by Truth

Page through the past 21 days either in this book or in your journal. Mark the areas which spoke loudest to your own story. Revisit those truths and present your struggles to God. Shake your dust off. Rise up and sit enthroned. Free yourself from the chains around your neck. Jesus came to free the captives and that means YOU. You are worth this life Jesus died to give you. Let His words sink deep into your heart. Get back on track if you need to. Celebrate the fact that God celebrates when His prodigal comes back home. You are good enough, you are smart enough and doggone it, people like you!

Day 22

There were six of us lying on the ground watching TV in our college apartment. We were as lively as amoeba (with my luck, I'll have a biologist tell me amoeba are actually quite active). After finishing our last set of finals, pure exhaustion took over. *Love Connection* had just ended and as the credits rolled, the announcer said, "If you live in the Los Angeles area, or if you will be visiting and you want to be on *Love Connection*, give us a call!"

It was like a bad idea simultaneously infected each of us. We perked up and finally showed signs of life. The banter started, "Wouldn't that be awesome if we all tried out, and they paid us money to date each other?" "Yeah, we could rig the system and be on the show together!" So we called. Audition times were set. We were having the time of our lives. Our interviews were held in a large room filled with lots of other singles. Some were obviously desperate to find a match. Others, like us, were there hoping for ten minutes of fame… although infamy was more like it.

I filled out the questionnaire with my typical sarcasm. What celebrity do I most resemble? Bill Cosby. Why do people want to date me? Because I can blow spit bubbles off my tongue (true story). It went on and on. The producers showed us old videos of past episodes. My favorite was when an African-American man sitting on the couch with Chuck Woolery said, "Chuck, she said she had great legs. Well, I've seen better legs in a bucket of Kentucky Friiiiiiiiiiied Chicken!"

Transformation by Truth

A few weeks passed and I forgot all about the show. I came home after a first date and checked my phone messages with my date standing next to me. Beep... "Hi Noelle! This is Jackie from *Love Connection*... We want you on the show! You'll be sitting next to Chuck on the couch, so please come in to watch the videos and choose your date!" Hmm. Note to self: don't check messages if you are not alone. Second note to self: if your college friends rope you into a TV show, there's always the chance that you will be the only one chosen. Third note to self: if you are the only one chosen, it's not as amusing.

The date with Bachelor Number Two was fun... even in the midst of threats from my parents, "Grandma Sase will be watching. Don't you dare do anything to embarrass us!" I planned the date and I was extra excited since the show was paying. But when I got my check for 40 dollars, I learned that "paying" was open to interpretation. After the date, we were instructed not to talk to each other until after our show taped. We were given a phone number to call so we could tell the producers about the date from our own perspectives.

I was immediately asked, "So, was it a love connection?"

"No, it was a friendship connection."

All of a sudden the tone changed, "Give me three reasons why you didn't like him."

"I never said I didn't like him. I said there was no chemistry."

"If there's no chemistry, there are reasons. Give me three."

It got to a point where we were at an impasse. I wouldn't say anything mean about Bachelor Number Two even when they egged me on by saying, "He said if you tried to hold his hand, he was going to throw up!" Since our story wasn't a steamy romance nor did it end in an ugly cat fight, we were told that they couldn't use us for the show. Well, that's what they *thought*.

Day 22

The couple they were going to use in our place must have really had a love connection, because they both came down with the mumps. So, we taped the show. For what it's worth, yes, the camera adds at least ten pounds ... and yes, I regret my Janet Jackson "Rhythm Nation" outfit. My date explained that things didn't quite work out since I was "too wholesome" for him. My parents were so excited that I didn't offend my Grandma Sase. But here's the comedy that I never considered until now: Grandma Sase didn't even speak English. Darn my parents were good...

APPLICATIONS

Heart:

This whole *Love Connection* experience symbolized the way I used to view love. I saw it as something nebulous that only a few were chosen to enjoy. It was a fleeting emotion that could go from passion to disgust in the span of 30 minutes. There was a chance it would be wonderful, but it could also be manipulative. It hurt. It was a crazy form of entertainment for some. And in most cases, you'd find that the one you loved didn't even speak the same language! That is Hollywood. But what does God say love is?

Love is patient, love is kind. It does not envy, it does not boast, it is not proud. It is not rude, it is not self-seeking, it is not easily angered, it keeps no record of wrongs. Love does not delight in evil but rejoices with the truth. It always protects, always trusts, always hopes, always perseveres. Love never fails... (1 Corinthians 13:4-8)

Chances are good that you've probably heard these verses recited at the majority of the weddings you've attended. But have you ever given serious thought to the concept? Think about scripture that instructs us to love such as Matthew 22:37-39 and 1 John 4:7. The hardest for all of us is probably Matthew 5:43-44 which says, *"You have heard that it was said, 'Love your neighbor and hate your enemy. But I tell you: Love your enemies and pray for those who persecute you.'"*

When I would hear or read those verses, I'd wait for God to give me warm fuzzies for my "enemy." Of course, that would never happen. On a really inspired day, I might go out of my way to say "Hi," thinking I was as close as I could possibly get to obeying those words that Jesus spoke. Have you ever been in those shoes?

Consider someone in your life who you could either classify as an enemy or someone who just plain irritates you. Instead of trying to manufacture warm fuzzies, list out each of the love actions that are in 1 Corinthians 13:4-7 (patience, kindness, etc.) in your journal. How can you apply those actions to your enemy? How does this differ from living by your emotions? Are you catching this? It's not about emotions or feelings. It's about action! With this renewed perspective, wouldn't you agree that it is more than possible to love your enemies? What can you do today to show more love to those around you: starting with those closest to you such as your family and friends and extending all the way out to your enemies? Journal your love plan.

Mind:

A fool's mouth is his undoing, and his lips are a snare to his soul. The words of a gossip are like choice morsels; they go down to a man's inmost parts. (Proverbs 18:7-8)

Day 22

I physically felt my blood pressure rise when the interviewer told me all of the mean-spirited remarks my date had supposedly said. "Your looks repulsed him. He was hoping for a beautiful blonde California babe." Wait a second. Since when am I not a blonde bombshell? Oh yeah, I'm the Japanese afro girl. Moving on.

My already fragile self-esteem was going downhill. My knee-jerk reaction was to fire offensive comments back. It's not that I wanted to hurt Bachelor Number Two. In fact, I liked him while we were on our date, and even as we taped the show we spoke highly of one another. But, in that moment, saying something rude about him would have made me feel better about myself.

Luckily, I knew that whatever I said would be broadcast to millions, so I refrained. But in an everyday situation, I can't guarantee that same type of bravado. Proverbs 18:7-8 says that my careless words will be my undoing. They are a snare to my soul. Words are so easily spoken, but they cannot be retracted. Not only do they hurt the recipient, but the underlying malicious spirit becomes a part of who I am, down to my inmost parts.

I'm assuming you're a lot like me. There have been times when you were the target of hurtful words that have had a lasting impact on your soul. On the other hand, you've also had moments that you're less than proud of because you carelessly spoke words that have hurt others. Maybe the words you spoke were flat out ugly. Or maybe you hid it well, justifying the gossip because it was in the spirit of "helping" a friend. However you dice it, you know in your heart of hearts if your words aren't constructive, they're destructive. Words hold immense power just like a surgeon's scalpel. If used incorrectly, it can kill. But when used correctly, it can heal someone's heart.

What is at least one practical step you can take to ensure your words will only be used to build others up and not tear them down? I have learned to press a pause button in my mind and make myself consider the long-term consequences before I speak. I'm not perfect, but I'm far better than what I used to be. If you have a laundry list of ideas, all the better. Journal your thoughts and put them in action.

Body:

I have said a million times (okay, a slight exaggeration) that one of the greatest blessings in my life was having heart failure at 28. After losing everything and then regaining the basic use of my body, I absolutely loved my body even when I could barely shuffle from my bed to the bathroom. I was finally comfortable in my own skin for the first time in my life. I had a profound sense of gratitude for the fact I could breathe without machines, I could sit up in my bed and I could walk over to pet my dog.

Have you ever been so convicted about something that you wanted to shout your message from a mountaintop? When I teach my fitness classes, I find myself preaching the same message, "Love what you've got! Even if you're nowhere near your goal, be grateful for your strong, amazing body."

As you can imagine, those words tend to fall on deaf ears. And if it weren't for my own experiences, I wouldn't be able to comprehend that message either. You might be thinking, "You want me to love my body? Can't you see that I am morbidly obese? What about those who have disabilities or a terminal disease?" How can I tell you to love your body when I don't know your story? Good point. So where do we

Day 22

go from here? I think the answer is still the same. Love your body. But use God's definition of love.

Today, how will you be patient with your body? How can you be kind to it? How can you appreciate the unique build God has given you instead of envying someone else's body? How can you refrain from being rude (think about the ways you speak about your body)? If you have exercised and dieted in the past and experienced numerous failures, how can you keep from being easily angered and keep no record of wrongs? What are the truths of your body that you can rejoice in? How will you protect it? How can you maintain your hope and perseverance? Love your body.

Choose at least one action step from 1 Corinthians 13:4-8 and love your body. What do you think? Write your thoughts in your journal. Love never fails!

Day 23

I've heard so many stories about little girls dreaming of their wedding days. Most of them sound something like this: a precious girl dresses in an oversized white dress; a dish towel covers her head to mimic a veil; humming the wedding march, she walks down a hallway in her home holding a bouquet of daisies freshly picked from a neighbor's yard; e-v-e-r-y detail is perfectly planned out. When I ask my friends, most of them say that they had similar fantasies of their own wedding days.

For me? Not so much. I never actually pictured my wedding day when I was little, but from the time I was six, I *did* know who my husband would be: either Shaun Cassidy or John Denver. Isn't God funny? Ryan is incredibly handsome and makes my heart skip a beat just as Shaun Cassidy did singing "Da Doo Ron Ron." And like John Denver, Ryan is a gifted musician, songwriter and vocalist. So God took my desires but gave me an even greater gift than what I thought I wanted.

The first time I actually started picturing what my wedding day would look like was shortly after Ryan and I got engaged. I didn't dream about the typical details like decorations, location or food. We knew we would have a simple, family-only, sentimental ceremony. Ryan's Mom had just died two months prior to our engagement and my parents were both losing their battles against cancer. So the details we struggled with revolved around my parents' presence or lack thereof at our ceremony. If we really rushed things, even my Mom, who we knew for sure was days away from dying, might be able to watch if we got married in their living room where her hospital bed was.

For a handful of reasons, this was not what God had in store for us. She went home to heaven in February, four months after Ryan's Mom. We decided on a March wedding to ensure my Dad's participation. I have always been a Daddy's girl, so having him there to give me away was extremely important. But he was not well. His heart was completely shattered without my Mom. To add to that anguish, his non-Hodgkin's lymphoma took over his body immediately after she left this earth. As our wedding day approached, my Dad was in isolation at the hospital enduring harsh treatments to prepare for a bone marrow transplant.

Our pastor gave us an idea: he and his wife would go with us to my Dad's bedside so he could officially give me to Ryan; and then we would go to the park to meet the rest of our family and complete our ceremony. I was blown away by God's plan. I played this through my mind for the few weeks that led to our big day. *How perfect* I thought. It *was* perfect until the day before our wedding when my Dad called me crying, "I am so sorry Noey. I cannot do this. My body just isn't strong enough. You and Ryan should just get married at the park." Calmly I replied, "Okay Dad, I understand. I love you, don't feel bad." As I hung up the phone, I melted down into a gut-wrenching cry. How could God do this to me?

Our wedding was lovely. My in-laws transformed the gazebo at the park with flowers and charming decorations. I even had rose petals scattered on the aisle I walked down. My beautiful sister was there to stand next to me. Ryan was as handsome as handsome gets. After we got married and celebrated at the park, our pastor and his wife went with me and Ryan to visit my Dad. You should have seen the smiles and

Day 23

teary-eyes that greeted us when people saw us coming down the hospital corridors. But, when we entered his room, it was like going from white to black. My Dad's eyes were closed. His face was swollen and pale. The room would have been silent if it weren't for the beeps coming from the machines that he was hooked up to. Our pastor Don touched my Dad's arm, put his face next to my Dad's and told him that I just got married. We leaned in close and Don prayed over all of us.

And then it happened. I was given the most heart-warming gift from my Dad and God. With valiant effort, my Dad opened his eyes, focused on me and spoke three powerful words I will cherish for a lifetime, "You look beautiful." His eyes shut and he fell back into his deep sleep.

APPLICATIONS

Heart:

As the heavens are higher than the earth, so are my ways higher than your ways and my thoughts than your thoughts. (Isaiah 55:9)

I'm sure you've found, like me, that things rarely go as planned. For the most part, I am okay with that. But there are times when I am convinced I am in the confines of God's will, or times when I truly believe I'm hearing Him speak to my heart... and then I get hit by an unexpected curve ball like the day before my wedding. My knee-jerk reaction is to pout and wonder why God disappointed me. Am I alone in my response? Can anyone shout "Amen!"?

And then I look at the Apostle Paul's life. He so badly desired to meet the Roman church to share his faith with them and to be encouraged by theirs. Certainly that must have been in God's will. He repeatedly persisted in asking God to open a way for that visit. *"I pray that now at last by God's will the way may be opened for me to come to you." (Romans 1:10)*

In my human understanding, I can't imagine why God wouldn't answer his prayers immediately. But, that wasn't the case, *"...I planned many times to come to you (but have been prevented from doing so until now)..." (Romans 1:13)* Well, since God closed those doors and said "No" to Paul's prayers, we have his written letter to the Romans which continues to teach and bless all of us today.

God did eventually open the door and He did answer Paul's prayer. But there was no red carpet rolled out for his travels. Instead, look at how God answered his prayers, *"My brothers, although I have done nothing against our people or against the customs of our ancestors, I was arrested in Jerusalem and handed over to the Romans." (Acts 28:17)* So Paul did get to Rome, but it was as a prisoner! Even though he was completely innocent of the charges, this was the avenue God used to send him to Rome. Unlike my pouty way of doing things, Paul chose to thankfully embrace the opportunity that God gave him. Under house arrest, Paul *"...welcomed all who came to see him. Boldly and without hindrance he preached the kingdom of God and taught about the Lord Jesus Christ." (Acts 28:30-31)*

Do you have areas in your life that are not going as planned? What will it take for you to submit to the fact that God's ways are higher than your ways? How can you transform your frustrated energy into faith? Journal your responses.

As for me, it's been ten years since I got married. My sister got married five years after I did. Had God given me my dream of having my Dad give me away, I would have had something that my sister would have sorely missed on her wedding day, since our Dad died 62 days after our Mom. I

Day 23

am so grateful that God closed that door for me. And those three words my Dad spoke? They still have an unexplainable, profound effect on my heart! I didn't know then, but God's ways truly were so far superior to mine.

Mind:

Things turn out best for the people who make the best out of the way things turn out. —Art Linkletter

What happens in your mind the moment your plans get derailed? Do you rebel by getting angry? If or when that occurs, where does your frustration take you? In other words, does it change the situation? If you cannot change the circumstances, all you have control of is your attitude.

Picture someone running on a treadmill. Do you think if they run faster they will get to a different destination? Obviously not. Think about that illustration if you get angry when things aren't going your way. You can get furious inside, but it doesn't change the facts. The circumstances still are what they are. So, what can you do to make the best out of the way things turn out? Journal your answer... and the more you can relate it to specific situations you face, the better off you will be.

Body:

One of the curveballs I struggle with most is when I am in a strong groove with my fitness and nutrition and then I either get sick or injured. Ugh, those times can feel defeating. Why Lord? You have shown me the value of being healthy and physically fit. Why did you allow this to happen?

Transformation by Truth

I was running in pain for about a year, absolutely fearful that if I went to the doctor I would be told I couldn't workout. Obviously it was not a smart choice to neglect my pain. In fact, it eventually got so severe that I was struggling to walk, so I finally went in. It was embarrassing to answer the question, "How long has this pain been going on?" I answered by saying, "I don't want to lie to you, but at the same time, I think you'd be better off not knowing the truth." Needless to say, I left that very day wearing a big ol' boot—I was now living my greatest fear.

But, here was what happened and this is where I want to encourage you. My doctor said, "You can't run. You can't jump rope. You can't do anything high-impact." You can't do this. You can't do that. After hearing his whole list, I asked, "So what *can* I do?" My doctor gave me a couple of ideas, and I got creative, researched and found for myself all the things I *could* do.

I could still do upper-body resistance training and upper-body cardio. I did boxing videos minus the legs; I could still ride a stationary bike and use the elliptical machine. Focus on what you *can* do! If you are limited in what you can do for your fitness and nutrition—whether it is your physical limitations, financial situation, time, children, or anything else—list those limitations in your journal. Next to each excuse… oops… did I say that out loud? Let me rephrase. Next to each hurdle, brainstorm creative solutions. If you need help, use Google or chat boards on health sites such as www.sparkpeople.com to get ideas. Keep this list close for the times when you need it. Commit today to not be upset when you face a turn in the road, but instead, enjoy the journey!

Day 24

    Two stories, one common denominator: Black Puffy Jacket (BPJ). I can't begin to tell you how much I love BPJ. Six years ago I found it in a small athletic outlet in the nearby mall for a mere twenty-dollar bill. Heaven knows that in Southern California, when the weather dips below 70 degrees, it's time to prepare for snow. So BPJ gets a lot of use. I wear it every morning at my winter session boot camp workouts. Anyone working out with me could describe me in one breath, "Little girl, big puffy jacket." I know what you are thinking, "If you love it so much, why don't you marry it?" Well, if I weren't married to Ryan, it would be a serious consideration.

    Many times on the weekends I drive 15 minutes down to Laguna Beach for a quiet time before my family wakes up. Believe it or not, it truly is parka weather down at the beach before sunrise. So, one particular Saturday, I dressed for the occasion. I teamed BPJ with Costco Ugg-like boots. Under BPJ was the ultra soft, sheer white t-shirt I woke up in. Since I never see anyone I know that early on weekend mornings, I dress for function, not for fashion. Ahh. Comfort and warmth. Heelloooooo Jesus!

    It's amazing to see and feel God's vast magnificence right on the sand with waves crashing in front of you. I savored every second of my prayer time, standing in awe and praise. Although I would have loved to stay, I knew that my time was running short since I could see the first signs of the sun's morning rays. I started back to my (very tough, extremely fierce) minivan, cupping my hands over my face so the air I exhaled would warm my nose. As I neared my van, I noticed a man waving at me. I waved back with a huge smile on my face. "Good morning!" I said with extra Christian cheer. He grumbled back, "Hey lady, I just wanted to let you know you have a flat tire."

Instead of waking Ryan up, I called roadside assistance. "No problem. We'll be there in 45 to 60 minutes." Yeah, right. When they showed up two hours later, they towed me 50 yards to a beachside mechanic. My van was fifth in line behind other cars that had been there from the night before. After sitting in the waiting area for over an hour, I eventually stepped outside into the direct morning sunlight to check in with Ryan. When I did, it was embarrassing to see the contrast between the way I was dressed compared to the bikinis and board shorts that now lined the sidewalk. So, I went back into the mechanics office to hide.

"Ma'am, do you want me to take your jacket for you? You must be boiling."

"Who me?" I asked as beads of sweat formed on my forehead, "No, I'm perfectly fine, but thank you."

Notice, I didn't mention a bra in my clothing description earlier because I wasn't wearing one. Not that my 12-year-old boy body needs support, but let's be real. The tight, sheer, white top would have caused a commotion of some sort. No, I couldn't part with BPJ. Maybe "love" is too strong of a word for that darn jacket.

Maybe not. Enter story number two which occurred one year later. The doorbell rang at 8:30 p.m. Just FYI, that happens to be my bedtime. I was already in flannel PJ bottoms and (you guessed it) a white, sheer, tight-fitting t-shirt. I ran into my office and listened to Ryan as he answered the door. The voice that responded was familiar. It was Ed, my friend

Day 24

who works out with me in the mornings. He was dropping by with a gift for one of the other boot campers. I stayed absolutely silent so he didn't know I was awake. I thought I was in the clear until I heard Ryan say the three words of death, "Please, come in!" My thoughts raced wondering what the heck my husband was thinking. Just then, I heard him holler, "Nooooeeeelle... Ed's here!"

Great. The hamsters running my brain went wild. I dropped my head down in defeat... and then I saw it on the floor... my beloved BPJ. My savior! I put it on quickly and zipped it up. I smiled and greeted Ed, who gave me that inquisitive look as if to say, "Is there ever a time you're not wearing your black puffy jacket?"

APPLICATIONS

Heart:

Have you ever found yourself in a rut that is so comfortable... it reminds you of BPJ? Comfortable? Yes. Totally effective? Probably not. It can get to a point where you do things without having a purpose. Have you ever found yourself wearing BPJ in your quiet times? Maybe you have gotten into a rut that looks something like this (read this with your best robot voice), "First I go to my kitchen table, then I read one chapter from the Old Testament, one chapter from the New Testament, one Psalm, one Proverb and then I pray for ten minutes..." For many years, that was my routine. And believe me, after my ridiculously structured Bible reading, I'd pray for ten minutes. Not 11, not 30 but ten. And then I realized it was so BPJ!

Transformation by Truth

See, I am doing a new thing! Now it springs up; do you not perceive it? I am making a way in the desert and streams in the wasteland. (Isaiah 43:19)

Although it's easier to get caught in your rut and repeat history, doesn't it excite you to know that God is doing a new thing in your life? You may have felt like you've been thirsty in a desert for quite some time now. God has a glistening, refreshing spring for you!

Nowadays, there seems to be cookie cutter approaches to everything, including how we worship our Lord. For me, I have to fight against my natural tendency to follow man-made patterns which leave me unfulfilled. I've grown to learn how to quiet the chatter in my head and let God weigh His thoughts on my heart and mind. Sometimes I realize God is calling me on a date in the park. Other times I feel led to spend time in a different room in my house. Sometimes music is involved, other times He speaks to me through books. I find that God is exciting... never boring!

How about you? Are you looking for God's new way in your desert? What is springing up? What does the stream in your wasteland look like? Your quiet times should be exciting and full of revelation. If they are, how will you maintain your awesome momentum? If they aren't, what needs to change? Journal your thoughts.

Mind:

We demolish arguments and every pretension that sets itself up against the knowledge of God, and we take captive every thought to make it obedient to Christ. (2 Corinthians 10:5)

Day 24

Maybe it's your mind that's clothed in BPJ. Think about it: when you are late for work and you are following a slow driver (who is in the fast lane), do you automatically get frustrated and feel your blood pressure rising? What happens when you wake up and find dirty dishes in the sink and you know that when you left the kitchen last, everything was spotless? Where does your mind go? Most of us get gridlocked in the same mental patterns day in and day out. What are the thoughts that occupy your mind throughout the day? Try this today: hold each thought captive. Captive? Say What? Whachu talkin' 'bout Willis? (Any Diff'rent Strokes fans out there?) Basically, think about what you are thinking about. Catch yourself and ask if that thought is what God would want occupying your mind. Work on making every thought "obedient to Christ."

The way to have a healthy, positive mindset is to strengthen it like you would your muscles. Flex your mind muscles! It's a change in perspective. Don't feel guilty for having negative or defeating thoughts, but realize what is in your mind and either change your perspective or proactively put in new thoughts. The more you do this, the more natural it will become. If you happen to be a "glass half-empty" person, this will feel really odd. But, keep on keepin' on! See the changes in your attitude. This will transform your daily life and bring incomparable joy. Make a commitment today to think about what you are thinking about. As you identify your patterns, journal them along with your ideas to make your mindset be "obedient to Christ."

Body:

If you just started becoming active, chances are good that you are not in any rut. But for those of you who have been working out for a while... ask yourself how varied your workouts are. I used to be queen of the same weight machines followed by 12 minutes of treadmill, then 12 minutes on the step climber e-v-e-r-y workout! What do you love to do? Have you tried videos or classes that are dance based? Or for us rhythm-challenged athletes (please tell me I'm not the only one), have you tried something different like a spin class? What about a hike, a bike ride, training for a race or taking up a new sport? Write down a list of ideas to shake things up and ink it into your calendar within the next week.

How about your eating? We tend to be creatures of habit. What can you do to keep your healthy eating exciting? My daughter and I have an ongoing Sunday afternoon date at the farmers market. We load up on organic, affordable produce as we stroll down each aisle looking for something new to try. Sierra loves to sample anything juicy and sweet. We have learned to love unique fruits and vegetables. Granted, we've also tried some real doozies, which we quickly spit out. But even those end up being a blessing in disguise because we end up sharing true belly laughs. You can find a farmers market near you at www.localharvest.org. Maybe you want to try and make a healthier version of a favorite food. Search online to redo some of your recipes. File the successes in your recipe box. What will you do to freshen up your health and wellness program? Write those thoughts in your journal.

No more BPJ!

Day 25

A sure-fire way to know I'm lagging on grocery shopping is seeing Ryan's tuna salad in a Tupperware on the second shelf of our fridge. That means that we are out of sandwich meat. So in his desperation, my honey gets a can of tuna from the pantry to make his lunch. I can hear it already, "I *wish* I had a husband who didn't complain if we were out of food. You should be so lucky that he comes up with his own solution!" Yeah, I get it. But hear me out. That tuna salad, which was the leftover from his lunch, will sit there in the same spot on the same shelf for *weeks*.

I have used every technique in the book to get him to change. I've been direct, "Ryan, are you going to finish this tuna or should I throw it out?" His reply is always, "Leave it there. I'll finish it." Seriously, that will still be his reply come week three. I have quietly moved his container right in front of something I knew he'd eat or drink. But he's like a mouse eating the peanut butter without triggering the trap. My last resort is always humor, "Ryyyaaaan! Your month-old tuna is asking for yooouu…" Nothing. In fact, I think it brings him pure joy to see me going out of my skull.

Now that I'm on a roll (Wouldn't that be hysterical if I were really sitting on a roll? Sourdough please!) let me tell you about Ryan and our debit card. I've only asked him a million times to give me the receipts so I can enter them into our Quicken ledger. When my head twists in full circles, he'll remember for the span of two transactions. That's it. Two times. After that, I have to go back to my passive-aggressive measures. I'll be online reviewing our bank account and in my critical way I'll say, "I see you ate at Philly's Best Sandwiches and spent nine dollars last Wednesday." Unfazed he says, "Yeah." He drives me N-U-T-S.

You know what else drives me nuts? His lack of grace with me. What? Who said "double standards"? One thing I'm really good at is coffee house recipe makeovers. A typical small-sized mocha has at least 150 calories, and the ingredients are not what you want to put into your body. My mocha is less than 25 calories, it doesn't contain any artificial sweeteners and it has antioxidants.

While all of my friends rave about my healthy drinks, do you know what Ryan says about it? As he's doing a white glove inspection (minus the white glove and it really isn't an inspection) where I measured out the cocoa powder and cinnamon, he'll rhetorically ask, "What happened? Did the dust fairy visit our countertops? I just cleaned them. Half of the cleanup is not making the mess in the first place."

Side note: I just read this out loud to Ryan. He said that I didn't come close to telling the whole story, "What about your lemons that you cut every morning on the counter? You don't use a plate or a cutting board. Your dust storm and drippings are *everywhere*! Are you planning to write about your disgusting socks that you ball up and throw in the laundry after running in wet grass at boot camp?" Okay, so maybe he has asked me more than a handful of times to take the extra second to unroll them and make sure they're right side out. But, do you know what I hear? Charlie Brown's teacher, "Waaah waaaah waaaahh…"

The funny thing is, I used to swear up and down that I'd never grow up to have my Mom's stubborn pride. In her opinion, you could do things her way… or… you could do things… *her* way. Am I turning into my Mom in some instances? Well… I am growing in grace each day… but I

Day 25

fully admit that the shoe seems to fit. So, feel free to call me Cinderella-san.

APPLICATIONS

Heart:

For in the same way you judge others, you will be judged, and with the measure you use, it will be measured to you.

"Why do you look at the speck of sawdust in your brother's eye and pay no attention to the plank in your own eye? How can you say to your brother, 'Let me take the speck out of your eye,' when all the time there is a plank in your own eye? You hypocrite, first take the plank out of your own eye, and then you will see clearly to remove the speck from your brother's eye." (Matthew 7:2-5)

How can you not laugh when you visualize yourself with a long plank of wood coming from your eye socket... and there you are, squinting and trying desperately to "help" someone get an invisible speck of dust from their eye? With this picture in my mind, I now ask God about the plank in my eye when I catch myself judging or condemning someone else's behavior. More often than not, I find that my frustration and my critical judgment is overbearing because the character flaw that is bothering me actually has a strong root in *me*. It's not that we aren't supposed to judge altogether, but we are called to correct ourselves first.

When you consider the people who you interact with on a regular basis, do you find that they have behaviors that drive you N-U-T-S? Journal your own situations and instead of asking God to fix the nutty people, ask God to reveal the planks that need to be removed from your eyes. What is God teaching you about *you*? Is He calling you to lighten up? To have more humor? To make big changes? To learn the lesson of perspective? To have more grace and forgive?

You might be in a place where you have asked God to reveal your planks, He has helped you remove them, and you now have to confront the speck of dust in someone else's eye. Jesus confronted. He confronted the issues while loving the people. Be ready to forgive (Ephesians 4:32) and speak the truth in love (Ephesians 4:15).

Write out what God reveals and what you're planning to do from here on, in response to His prompting. I know for me, the Lord is certainly working in my heart on many different levels. In the spiritual world, I must look hysterical with all those wood beams coming from my eyes. Do you think I could supplement my income by selling my stories including pictures of logs coming out of my eye sockets to the *National Inquirer*? Wishful thinking I guess…

Mind:

Our minds can be a playground for spiritual attacks. Something can be as silly as old tuna salad and the next thing you know, negative messages bombard your mind saying, "He *always* does this. He's not being very thoughtful. Why doesn't he love me the way I love him?" And then you find yourself searching for more proof to make your point stronger. "If he respected me, he'd remember the debit receipts. I don't remember him kissing me when I got home from work…" There are times when I get so worked up because one little thing snowballed as I agreed with all those condemning thoughts in my mind. Ryan will ask me, "What was the

Day 25

reason for this argument again? I forgot." Inevitably I don't remember either, but I hate to admit it. So I'll give him a silent treatment as I jog my memory trying to recall exactly what it was *he* did to cause this war. Ryan, on the other hand, will be cracking up, doing a one-man-conga dance trying to get me to lighten up.

Can you think of instances where you were busy compiling evidence for your case because you wanted to be right instead of being well? Consider that the enemy works overtime to put those thoughts into your head. Take a moment to reflect on the fact that there will be a day when those irritants won't be in your life. For me, it'll be a very sad day if Ryan leaves this earth before me and I have a sparkling clean fridge. I will yearn for the days when his month-old tuna was on that second shelf. What can you do differently with this knowledge? Journal your thoughts including solutions you can implement.

Body:

"I can't eat well because my spouse keeps junk food in the pantry." "I don't have time to exercise because my job is so demanding." "My family members told me that I'll just put the weight back on like usual." "You have no idea what my culture is like. It revolves around unhealthy food!" "I keep the Oreos for the kids. It's not my fault I have that weakness once everyone goes to bed." "If I don't eat my mother-in-law's cooking, she'll be offended." "I've tried a million different diets and nothing works." "The economy is so bad, I cannot afford to eat well or exercise." "Someone brings donuts to the office every day."

Arrrggggghhhhhh! Really? I mean… *really*? Confessions of a fitness trainer… this is only a small sampling of what I hear. Notice that in each complaint, the blame is on something or someone else. There is no personal ownership of their situations or choices. Sure, I would love to blame someone or something else for my problems as much as the next person. But, whenever we do, we lose all of our power. Write your health-related excuses in your journal. What control do you have in each excuse? If you don't have control, you cannot fix the problem and if you can't fix it, it does no good to complain about it. What actions are you committed to take so you can move toward your physical goals?

Here's an example: "I can't eat well because my spouse keeps junk food in the pantry." Psst... Ryan, this is purely hypothetical, honey. *I* have control over my healthy choices that *I* keep in the pantry. *I* can ask Ryan... I mean "my spouse"... to keep his Lay's potato chips and Pop Tarts in the part of the pantry that only he can reach. *I* can commit to three minutes of jump roping before *I* make my snack choices.

Work on you. Get the plank out. Forget about the speck of dust.

Day 26

I love baths. I stack up a handful of magazines on one corner of the tub and a glass of ice-cold water with lemon wedges on the other. When I come out looking like a Japanese dried plum, you know I'm having a great day. January 24, 2003 was one of those pruned-up, great days. Although I only had one magazine to read, there was an article that grabbed my heart. It was a story of a family's journey to adopting their daughter from China. Not only did this story move me, it changed me. I got out of the bath soaking wet with my magazine in hand and interrupted Ryan's guitar playing and read him the story. Both of us were teary-eyed and Ryan said, "We're adopting from China, aren't we?"

When Ryan had asked me to marry him, I was so humbled by the honor of taking his name and becoming a Dey. Once we became our own family, we had the ability to give this same gift to a baby. I couldn't believe there would be an appointed time when we would welcome a precious new Dey! Along with the excitement though, came 15 months of paperwork, adoption home studies, meetings with our social worker and preparation to become parents.

I can't say that those months were the easiest time for us. I'd get frustrated with the tedious nature of the paperwork and Ryan tried to reconcile going from the guy who never wanted to get married and never wanted to have kids to seeing God's gifts of becoming a husband and a dad-to-be. It was plain to see that we had very separate issues when I overheard Ryan's end of a phone conversation telling a friend, "No, the paperwork's not that hard." Holy cow! I gave him the ultimate stink eye. I can still hear my shriek, "It's not hard because *I do it all for you and tell you where to sign*!"

I struggle with patience. Ryan, not so much. He knew that God had His perfectly appointed time for us to become parents. I, on the other hand, became addicted to Chinese adoption chat groups and constantly checked the China Center of Adoption Affair's website. I knew exactly when our referral would be sent to our agency. I had my cell phone attached to my hip. With all of that micro-management, don't ask me how I missed *the* call.

I was in my home office. I looked at my phone and saw, "Missed call from Sabrina." Ryan was in the kitchen. I ran to him, my voice shaking and said, "She called!" Standing together, I called Sabrina back.

She answered the phone saying, "Noelle..."

My words were barely audible, "Am I a mom, Sabrina?"

"Congratulations! You and Ryan have the most beautiful 18-month-old baby girl!"

Months before this life-changing moment, we knew our daughter's name would be Sierra Dey since both of us grew up in the beauty of Lake Tahoe's Sierra Nevada mountain range during summer vacations. And whatever her Chinese name was, we committed to keep it as her middle name to show our deep respect for her personal history. Within a few hours of our phone call, we were sitting in our adoption agency waiting for Sabrina's arrival. She battled Friday night Los Angeles traffic so we could see Sierra's picture for the first time. When she came through the door, I grabbed Ryan's hand as I literally trembled. When Sabrina opened the manila file, we saw her. Her beauty was stunning. She had perfect little fingers, big eyes, a teeny nose and a hint of a knowing grin.

Day 26

Moms who have physically given birth all tell me similar stories. I'll ask them how painful their delivery was and they'll say, "I endured pain, but the moment I saw my baby for the first time, I was on such a spiritual high, the pain faded to the background." That same principle held true for our adoption. The moment we laid eyes on her, everything leading us to that point vanished.

Only in God's perfect intimacy could so many miracles be woven into our story. They estimate Sierra's birthday to be January 31, 2003. That would have been exactly seven days after we read the magazine article. Seven is God's number of perfect completion. And, January 24, 2003 was not only the day Sierra was born in our hearts, but it was also my Dad's birthday. It was the first one we had without him here since he went to heaven the year before. On a day that could have easily been filled with loss, God transformed it into a day of the most incredible, eternal gain. And since Sierra was found during Chinese New Year, her Chinese name Xiao Xin translates into "a new dawn" or "a new day." Are you kidding me?! Yes! *She is A NEW DEY!*

APPLICATIONS

Heart:

When Ryan first laid eyes on his little girl's picture, a new song was being written in his heart. "One Girl" speaks to his journey of becoming the man God created him to be. Ryan would pray and ask God to help him be more selfless. Since God is... well... *God*... Ryan wondered what measures the Lord would take to answer his prayers. To Ryan's astonishment, his prayers were answered by a miracle.

Transformation by Truth

> *God can rain down fire from heaven*
> *Throw a mountain in the sea*
> *Do away with world hunger*
> *He can cure all disease*
> *He can raise the dead to living*
> *He can calm a raging storm*
> *He can stop all pain and suffering*
> *Bring an end to every war*
> *And God can change a heart with just one girl*

"One Girl" – Ryan Dey

I used to think miracles were only the awesome stories of God raising Lazarus from the dead or parting the Red Sea. And while God is more than capable of doing these types of miracles, Ryan's song lyrics point out that some of the biggest miracles God performs are the miracles of changed hearts. God changed Ryan's heart and answered his prayer with a 19-pound miracle and she was *made in China!*

What about you? Can you use a change-of-your-heart-miracle? You actually have all the makings right where you are, just as you are. God shines His light of revelation. Are you willing to open your eyes to it? Are you aware that *you* are a miracle? Psalm 139:14 explains that you are fearfully and wonderfully made. God actually knitted even your most delicate, inner parts inside your mother's womb (Psalm 139:13). The New Living Translation describes you as wonderfully complex and a marvelous workmanship! Is that hard for you to believe? It's probably not a stretch to comprehend those words for someone you love deeply, right? But what about *you?*

Day 26

Can you imagine holding a baby for the first time, getting eye contact and whispering, "Hello little one. You have a blank slate for this life of yours! I hope you find a job where you can fly under the radar and survive paycheck to paycheck."? Of course not! You look into the baby's eyes and you know that this miracle can change our world. Well, you are still that miraculous little baby even though you have some years behind you now.

In your prayer time, ask God to reveal the miracle of you. Are you having a hard time believing what Psalm 139:13-14 says about you? If so, journal what it is that is holding you back from complete belief. Lift all of your pain, anguish, fear, regrets... everything that is keeping you from living your miraculous life. Lift it all to God and, in faith, stand with me in prayer and ask Him to replace those emotions with His strength, peace, revelation and wisdom. Write about the life that you need to start living because YOU (insert your name here) are a marvelous workmanship! YOU are wonderfully complex! YOU are fearfully and wonderfully made!

Mind:

Stand up and walk out of your history. –Dr. Phil

Think about your life's story. Or, said another way, think about your history. If I was having coffee with you, how would you tell your story? Sierra is now nine years old and she has a deep, passionate heart. She'll tell you that her life is a story about God's love for her and her parents. Out of all the babies in the whole world, God chose to pick her out and pair her with us even though we were on opposite sides of the world. Now, being realistic, I understand that she could also view her life with a different perspective. She could explain how tragic her story is since she lived in an orphanage for the first 20 months of her life. Facts are facts, but how you choose to *use* those facts creates your story.

Think about that. Why is it that some people can endure horrific abuse, suffer life-limiting diseases, be surrounded by death and dying… yet when they tell you their story, it's filled with inspiration and victory? And then there are those who have had a pretty easy life, relatively speaking, and after they share their history with you, you feel exhausted and you're compelled to limit your time with them. Which type of person will you choose to be? Is your story a love story? Is it drama-filled? Is it a tragedy? Is it an adventure? Do you need to "stand up and walk out of your history"?

Write your story in your journal. Don't feel bad if you've been living a drama-filled life or if you've been an energy zapper to those around you. Well, I should say, don't feel bad if that's your beginning. It's time to write the present and the future. Everyone loves a movie where there is a stunning transformation. Consider movies where the underdog comes from behind to claim victory. Or, how about the movies where the bad guy turns into a good guy at the end? Any of those inspiring stories can be yours. So, write or re-write your history and live the miracle!

Body:

After the baby is delivered, the mom's pain fades to the background and all she focuses on is her new precious gift. When you look at your exercise plan and nutrition, where is your attention? Are you crabby because your muscles are sore

Day 26

from your last workout? Do you get angry when you see your friends eating fried-heaven-knows-what while your plate is filled with veggies, fish and quinoa? Are you thinking, "Hey lady, what's kwin-o-uh?" Uh yeah, it's keen-wah... the super grain, Google it. Anyhow, back to the point. What will it take for you to focus on the end result knowing full well that everything leading up to it will all pale in comparison? Write your plan and live it!

Day 27

After we received Sierra's picture and her background information, I went shopping and made a special care package to send to our new daughter. The box we shipped had a Winnie the Pooh stuffed bear, the softest pink blankie I could find, our wedding photos and a CD of Ryan's music. We contacted her orphanage through our Chinese-American advocates. My first email was filled with questions asking about Xiao Xin's (Sierra's) day-to-day life: her likes, dislikes and what her little personality was all about.

Within a day, the orphanage director and nannies responded by saying, "Xiao Xin loves music and sweet food. She's a bit of a trouble maker though. She's often found stealing other children's toys. But, she has a deep love for her crib mate named Wen Wen. Xiao Xin spends her days taking care of Wen Wen by giving her all the toys she takes from others."

I analyzed every word in the email. She was obviously Ryan's daughter since she had a love of music, she was a trouble maker and liked to eat sweets. The only trait she showed that was mine was the way she cared for her friend (Humble Living 101 by Noelle Dey).

When the time came for us to travel to China to unite with our daughter a couple months later, the thought of Sierra being separated from Wen Wen tore my heart. I worried that Sierra would miss her dear friend, but that concern paled in comparison to my fear of Wen Wen being left behind wondering where her big sister went.

We traveled from Los Angeles to Beijing with three other families. Two of those families were heading to the same province as us to unite with their babies. As we rode in the shuttle to the adoption office in Nanjing, our interpreter Mona explained, "Two of your babies are already there waiting for you. Ryan and Noelle, Xiao Xin is not there yet because her orphanage is further away and they've been driving through the countryside. She's been on a six-hour car ride with another baby, two nannies and the director of the orphanage." Surprisingly, I really didn't care that we had an extra wait because my heart was still fixated on Wen Wen's loss.

Since Ryan and I still had a half-hour wait, we were able to capture the other families "Gotcha!" moments on video. It was literally priceless to watch the families welcome their newest members with such elation. After a while, Ryan said, "Don't you think it's about time? Let's go wait by the doors." As we stared through the double glass doors, we watched a white van pull up. There were two tiny shadows and three larger ones. Nervously I whispered, "I think that's her... there's two orphans and three caretakers!" As they approached us, we called out, "Xiao Xin!" The nanny didn't hand her to us until Mona spoke in Chinese, pointed to us and said, "Xiao Xin. Mama, Dadda." We were handed Sierra Xiao Xin Dey. Nineteen pounds never felt so wonderful.

Time stopped. Although there was conversation all around us, I couldn't hear anything except for Ryan and the tiny little voice I now recognized as our daughter's. But just then, one more voice entered my world. The director of the orphanage was talking to our interpreter. I couldn't understand anything she said until... I heard two words. I couldn't believe my ears, "Wen Wen." I looked behind me and asked Mona, "Please find out if this is the same Wen Wen that was

Day 27

Sierra's special friend at the orphanage." It was! She was going to be adopted in two hours. I quickly wrote a heartfelt letter to her family-to-be. I explained the special relationship our girls shared. It didn't matter where in the world Wen Wen was going, I just wanted the girls to have the opportunity to find one another again.

We were pulled away from all of the other families to meet with the government officials. After signing papers and verbalizing our intent, Sierra Xiao Xin was released to us for one day. The very next day we would sign our official adoption papers. Sierra Xiao Xin and Wen Wen closed one chapter of their lives and turned the page with parents who were beyond blessed to take them into their predestined "forever families."

APPLICATIONS

Heart:

For he chose us in him before the creation of the world to be holy and blameless in his sight. In love he predestined us to be adopted as his sons through Jesus Christ, in accordance with his pleasure and will— to the praise of his glorious grace, which he has freely given us in the One he loves. (Ephesians 1:4-6)

As Sierra grows older, she will have a deeper understanding of the undeniable love that went into her adoption. Ryan and I yearned for her. God put a desire deep in our hearts that only she could fill. Her birth mother had the courage to bring her pregnancy to full term. She safely placed her tiny baby, perfectly wrapped in a blanket, on the west side of a busy market knowing she would certainly be found and she would be cared for until our arrival. Love encompasses every side of Sierra's story.

Just the same, you were chosen before God made this world to be adopted into His own family. He yearned for you. Through Jesus, you are faultless in God's eyes. You bring him joy and pleasure!

In addition to this miraculous story of Sierra, I distinctly remember my visits to the local animal shelter where I adopted my two dogs. Oh how they grabbed my heart. I could watch them play and cuddle with them all day long. They bring me such joy! In your journal, explain what adoption means to you. How does the knowledge of your adoption into God's family impact your self-esteem? What will you do differently today with that knowledge?

Mind:

Do you want to do something beautiful for God? There is a person who needs you. This is your chance. —Mother Theresa

Countless times I've been asked, "How did you travel to China and only adopt one, knowing there were so many more babies that needed homes?" Sometimes I laugh thinking God must have used my feelings of being overwhelmed to protect my heart since all I could focus on was Sierra. In almost every area of my life, I'm a multi-tasker, whereas Ryan reminds me he's a guy, "a one-trick pony." Well, thankfully I became a one-trick pony in China because if that question had been rooted in my mind, I easily could have been overcome with the sorrow surrounding me, to the point where I couldn't help anyone.

Without making a laundry list of people who need you, can you focus on just one today? What are you willing to do

Day 27

to "do something beautiful for God?" Who needs you? Write in your journal what you are planning to do with your chance.

Body:

Have you ever felt alone... in a place where no one understands you... to the point where you feel like an abandoned orphan? Undoubtedly, in our lives we will endure pain and suffering. Here's the deal: we cannot control many of these circumstances. However, we do have control over what we eat, drink and how we respect our bodies.

It's not uncommon for people to turn to food addictions in these lonely times. Food turns into medication or a reliable friend. It doesn't have a negative stigma like alcohol, drugs or smoking, so it's incredibly common. Do you turn to God for comfort during the low periods of your life, or do you turn to food or other vices? Do you eat or drink in hiding? Do you binge, purge or refrain from eating altogether? Have you gained or lost substantial amounts of weight right after a tragedy? Do you bargain with yourself or with God? Many people will say, "I'll eat this now, but workout extra hard tomorrow."

When this occurs, ask, "What is the underlying hunger? Am I depressed, hopeless or stressed? Is my true hunger love, acceptance, affirmation...?" Using a concordance at the back of your Bible, do a search for that need. You can also use Google to find Bible verses on your particular topic or search a topical Bible (I like using the online topical Bible at www.openthebible.info). Write out the scriptures that apply to your *spiritual* hunger. For instance, when I feel like no one understands me, I will hold tight to Psalm 34:17-18 which says, *"The righteous cry out, and the LORD hears them; he delivers them from all their troubles. The LORD is close to the brokenhearted and saves those who are crushed in spirit."* I'll also saturate my heart and mind with 2 Corinthians 1:3-4, *"Praise be to the God and Father of our Lord Jesus Christ, the Father of compassion and the God of all comfort, who comforts us in all our troubles..."*

Write your verses in your journal and ask God to reveal Himself through them. How do His words of hope and understanding apply to your situation? What does God want you to do on a practical level to implement His wisdom? Maybe you'll seek out counseling, maybe He'll heal your heart with the words you found in the Bible, or maybe you'll be drawn to a book that addresses your struggles. There are countless ways God can mend your brokenness. Take the time to wait on His answers. Keep on this journey of seeking His truth for a lifetime. These steps will address the underlying deep wounds that only God can heal.

You'll also need "band-aids" which represent your plan for using healthier alternatives to replace your current destructive behaviors. I know that when my emotions go haywire, I crave sweets and a bag of Flamin' Hot Cheetos. So, I have proactively taken out those tempting foods from our home. When those times hit, I remove myself from the kitchen. Instead, I can pamper myself with a homemade spa. I take a hot bubble bath and sip a glass of water with a lemon wedge. Or I can watch TV or read upstairs away from the kitchen. Sometimes I need to get away from the house altogether. I can go for a walk in the park with my dog Digger. What would work for you? Can you call a friend? Take up a new hobby? Write your plan. How will you implement this now? I'm not talking about tomorrow, not next time, but now!

Day 28

When I met Ryan months before we started dating, he had a ten-year-old pickup truck with a lot of character. It had 230,000 original miles and you could tell it was part friend, part transportation and part home. Part home? Well, at least part kitchen. The first time he gave me a ride in it, he had to clear some space for me to sit down. McDonald's wrappers and empty coffee cups blanketed the seats and floor board. So, it seemed rather fitting that after we left the adoption office with Sierra, our first family meal would be at McDonald's in China. Actually, we ate every meal there aside from our group dinners since it was the only restaurant where we felt safe ordering without an interpreter.

The next morning we woke up as a family of three. It was surreal giving Sierra a bath and getting her dressed in the pink and denim Old Navy outfit we received at my baby shower. I could hardly believe it was our official adoption day. When we were back in the adoption office, I asked Mona if Wen Wen and her family would be there with us. They would, but only for a bit.

I introduced myself to Gina, Wen Wen's beautiful Mom. Like us, her world was turning upside down... or better said... right side up. Wen Wen, now named Alayna, melted into her Mom's arms. I wanted to have meaningful conversations with Gina, but there weren't any opportunities with all of the nervous energy around us. My heart was settled though since she had all of my contact information. I felt certain she would get in touch with me when we all got back to America.

Nearly a year went by and she never contacted me. So many questions consumed my mind. I wondered if I had overstepped my boundaries. Sporadically I would relive the words I hurriedly wrote to her. Were they offensive? Did she feel uneasy with our family since she looked to be a single mom? Was it just time to close that chapter of Sierra's life?

It was a run-of-the-mill September day and I logged into my AOL account. I just about lost my breath as I opened an email from Gina. Her words carried a flood of emotions. I couldn't pinpoint my feelings, but tears drenched my face as I read, "I just uncovered the beautiful letter you wrote to me... That time in China was such a struggle. I had to travel alone since my husband stayed behind to take care of our special needs daughter Natalee... I desperately wanted John, or at least someone around me to help, but I was alone with a new baby and I was completely overwhelmed. We would love to see you!"

Wow, what a lesson in humility. I had made that year of silence all about *me*! I felt like I was stuck on a treadmill in my head. Endless thoughts were constantly running, but I was going nowhere. My mind was plagued as I second guessed every one of my good intentions. Since I chose the path of obsession, I missed the opportunity to take that energy and lift Gina and Alayna up in prayer.

The Dunns are a close-knit family founded firmly in God's love. They live in Arizona, our neighboring state. We stayed in contact by emails, phone calls and shared pictures. Then four years after we had last seen one another in China, Gina explained that they were preparing for a vacation to San Diego, which is only an hour drive for us, "Is there any way

Day 28

you can come down so the girls can reunite?" As we were driving, we asked Sierra if she remembered Alayna, "You would have known her as Wen Wen." Sierra said she thought so, but she wasn't quite sure.

We pulled into the parking lot and saw their family. My tears flowed uncontrollably as we all waved and smiled. Getting out of the car, I held tightly to Sierra's hand and we walked toward our newly extended family. Gina gave me the biggest hug as Ryan and John met each other for the first time. We looked at our girls. Both were silent and mirrored one another's stone face. They gave each other the up-and-down glance; similar to the kind of stare that we women hate receiving when we pass by a cheesy guy. But, before we could intervene, they had grabbed hands, ran to the park and were inseparable the entire day.

We promised that we would not only keep in touch, but we would make it a point for the girls to see each other as much as possible. The next year we stayed at their house for a mini getaway. After the girls went to bed, Gina and I stood in the doorway and watched them sleep. It hit us hard as we tried to grasp the enormity of God's perfect plan. God protected Sierra and Alayna by giving each of them the gift of the other. They slept in the same crib and grew up together for 17 months of their lives. Once their families were prepared, He handpicked the girls and perfectly placed them in loving Christian homes that were only separated by a six-hour drive. In that moment in time I remember Gina whispering, "If China could only see... Here we are five years later and our girls are peacefully sleeping together... *again*!"

APPLICATIONS

Heart:

"For I know the plans I have for you," declares the LORD, "plans to prosper you and not to harm you, plans to give you hope and a future." (Jeremiah 29:11)

Can't you just hear God's voice whispering those words to our girls in their orphanage? His words were truth. Both girls are now nine years old and are prospering in personality and in love. They have amazing futures in a land of opportunity and freedom. They live in homes where God's love reigns. His care for their stories is so intricate that He would hand pick them and give them new families at the exact same time so neither was left behind, not even for a moment. He gently placed them over 6,000 miles away from their birth country, yet their homes would only be separated by a six-hour drive.

But if you think of their story from only a human perspective, what would the odds be that they would have thriving lives? Taking only the facts, things didn't look good. They were born female into a male-dominated society. They were abandoned at birth. Many orphans go to foster homes where they learn to bond and how to love. Our girls stayed at their orphanage where the child-to-staff ratio made it difficult for them to get the affection, eye contact and attention that the caretakers would have desired.

But God…

But God knew the plans He had for them. But God planned to prosper them and not harm them. Are you facing a challenge today where the odds are completely stacked

Day 28

against you? Write out Jeremiah 29:11 in your journal. Take time to really let those words sink into your heart and mind. How does this change your perspective? Write your prayer responding to this message God is speaking to you.

Mind:

Life isn't about how to survive the storm but how to dance in the rain.
— Author Unknown

For John and Gina, this was their second adoption. Five years before Alayna, they had adopted Natalee. God had given John and Gina a very special desire to give their hearts and their home to a healthy Chinese baby. When their moment of "giving birth" took place, they excitedly opened their referral picture with anticipation. They looked at their precious daughter with overwhelming adoration. She was two years old; significantly older than they expected, but they quickly adjusted their desires. As a first time Mom, Gina tenderly studied Natalee's photo. But there was something in her maternal heart that was left a bit unsettled, "Something doesn't look quite right." John tried to reassure her by explaining, "Underneath that sad face is a happy girl."

For the first two years after her adoption, Natalee didn't talk aside from speaking the words "Mama" and "Dadda." She couldn't seem to focus when her parents interacted with her. When I asked Gina what was going through her mind, she said, "I kept thinking that our love would fix her. We were committed to do whatever God called us to do for this sweet child." It wasn't until she was nine when they met with a gifted and compassionate neurologist who explained that Natalee is autistic. Gina said she broke down. Although

Natalee was tagged as a "special needs" child shortly after they left China, the diagnosis of autism broke her. She had no idea.

I met Natalee when our families reunited shortly after this diagnosis. After our day picnicking, we took the kids to Balboa Park. Sierra and Alayna went on the kids' rides, but Natalee's only desire was to go on the big rollercoaster. John took her while the rest of us watched the younger girls. I voiced my surprise to Gina, "I can't believe Natalee isn't afraid of those steep hills!" It turns out she lives for that adrenaline rush. Since her neurons don't fire correctly, it takes extreme excitement to stimulate certain parts of her brain. She walked off the ride and immediately asked if she could go on it again—this time she invited me. I sat next to her in awe. I've never seen such a joyful smile on anyone's face in my entire life.

Natalee taught me that I can mentally choose to embrace the rollercoaster of my life just as she does… just as John and Gina do… or I can fear every turn and hill. What is the rollercoaster in your life? What will it take for you to submit to God by putting your hands in the air, letting go of your controlling nature and embrace the ride like the Dunn family? How can you let John and Gina's testimony impact your journey? Journal your thoughts.

Body:

Ah yes. Me. The clean eater. I ate at the McDonald's in Nanjing everyday. Of course McDonald's is not somewhere I would ever choose to eat. But there are those random times in life when I find myself at an unhealthy restaurant or a fast food chain. Has this ever happened to you? List all of the restaurants and fast food joints that you go to. I'm not there to

Day 28

see your journal, so be honest! Google the nutritional information and choose a couple of items at each of the restaurants that fit into your eating plan. Most chain restaurants have their information available at their locations, but I highly recommend you make your decisions before you arrive. Commit to eat the healthier options you researched and pass on the emotional impulse items.

What about the food you really, really love? Brainstorm your ideas for items that you don't want to live without. Can you give your special recipes a healthy makeover? If not, how can you change your portions? What other ideas can you think of so you stay on track with your health and fitness goals? Journal and execute!

End of Week 4:

> *"I'm strong to the finich*
> *Cause I eats me spinach..."* – Popeye

Sadly, as you have seen, I'm incredibly brilliant when it comes to 70's television. You would guess I was a latchkey kid, but I actually had a stay-at-home Mom who was completely integrated in my life. Needless to say, I remember watching Popeye cartoons early on Saturday mornings.

Think about Popeye for a moment. He didn't care much for grammar, he had an eye deformity, his forearms were way out of proportion to the rest of his body, he loved and he had an adversary. Doesn't that sound like any of us? We all have our random idiosyncrasies, our bodies are unique, we love God, we love others, and we have an enemy. I love how Popeye didn't obsess over his body's imperfections. He himself would say, "I yam what I yam." He fought the good fight. But, inevitably, he would find himself in some serious binds. Can't you just picture Brutus pinning Popeye down? So, how did Popeye respond?

He remembered how to tap into his strengths. For him, it was his can of spinach. For us, we have God living in us. What?! Can you grasp that? Because for me, it's nearly impossible to comprehend that the same God who raised Jesus from the grave... the God who created the heavens and the earth by His spoken word... He is living in me! He is living in YOU!

I am prayerful that you have an understanding of the immense power and love that is literally *in* you. That can of spinach is in your grasp. Are you going to squeeze it, ingest

Transformation by Truth

it and be a powerhouse for truth? Or are you going to leave it in your back pocket and get caught belly-up with Brutus breathing his hot air over your face? Unfortunately, most will live conforming to the patterns of this world. Brutus is on top of them. Their spinach is right there, but they choose to get pummeled instead.

But you? No way.

Do not conform any longer to the pattern of this world, but be transformed by the renewing of your mind. Then you will be able to test and approve what God's will is—his good, pleasing and perfect will. (Romans 12:2)

Whenever you feel like you are conforming to the patterns of this world, stop in your tracks. Renew your mind by nourishing your heart, mind and body with God's truths. His good, pleasing and perfect will for your life is for you to shine. Take a moment to revisit your goals. With a freshly renewed mind and by the power of the Holy Spirit guiding your thoughts, do you need to tweak some of your ways? Or are you right on track with your heart, mind and body goals? Journal your thoughts. Be strong to the finich! Grab your spinach!

Day 29

When Sierra started first grade, she wanted to be an artist when she grew up. I loved the family portraits she used to draw. Inevitably we were missing our arms and feet; Ryan was shorter than me; and on a rare occasion, our eyelashes were where our eyebrows should have been (either that, or we were all in a desperate need to be plucked). So when her school announced that they were proudly presenting "Art Masters Night," an evening where our children's artwork would be framed and on display for purchase, we were all excited to go.

It was really a great fundraiser. The aisles were set up in a way where the kids must have felt like they were walking through a museum. My favorite part of the evening was seeing the satisfaction on Sierra's face when she found her own painting which had been transformed by being matted and framed since she saw it last. After several minutes of us doting over Sierra and her masterpiece, Ryan took her painting off of its stand and we stood in line to pay.

On our way out, a PTA mom had asked us if we had checked out the activity center. It turned out, there was a room where Sierra could do a hands-on project. There were a couple of parents helping our kids make holiday pop-up cards. Sierra's eyes grew big when she saw all of the sparkly paint pens. The volunteering mom at the craft table showed Sierra the selection of cards she could choose from. I didn't look at everything, but I saw one that had a turkey on the front for Thanksgiving and another card had a Christmas tree. As she was taking her time to decide, Ryan and I took a few steps back and got caught up on one another's day.

My focus quickly shifted away from my conversation with Ryan when I heard the mom say to Sierra, "Wow! You're the *first* person to choose this card!" Okay, that grabbed my attention. With all the kids that had already come through to do this craft, I wondered what she chose. Ryan and I looked over Sierra's shoulder to see a card with seven candles and the banner, "Happy Kwanzaa!" Ryan and I got eye contact with the mom and it took everything we had to not crack up.

The next morning, I dropped Sierra off at school in the light rain. After walking her to class, I was hurrying through the parking lot to get to my van. Parents can get a little crazy in our school's parking lot, but there was a driver nice enough to let me cross. I waved to thank her, and then I noticed it was the volunteering PTA mom from the night before. With that recognition, I started *really* waving—you know what I mean, right? I'm talking make-a-rainbow-with-my-arm wave. No reaction back.

I quickly realized I looked nothing like I did the night before. She would have remembered me if I had been dressed up in work clothes with my hair done and if I had my make-up intact. But that was so last night. Fast forward to the scene in the parking lot where I became the in-the-rain-rainbow-waver. I was in a sweaty workout outfit, my hair was in a ponytail and I had no make-up. In other words, I took the grunge look to a new level. So what did I do? I found myself *yelling* (everyone's windows were up, it was a rainy day) with even bigger hand gestures, "Hey! It's me, the Kwanzaa lady!" Nothing. At least, not from her.

Do you know the feeling when you can literally feel the weight of people staring at you? Yeah... me too. It was coming from all the other parents who were walking in the parking lot. Holy guacamole. Did I just yell, "It's me, the

Day 29

Kwanzaa lady?" Really? That was the best way I could describe myself? As if it even mattered. The moment I got into my van, I sat there paralyzed and thought that life would be so much easier if I could just learn to let things go. The Kwanzaa lady? Come on Noelle. Ugh!

APPLICATIONS

Heart:

I wish I could say this obsessive moment was an isolated incident. But that would be like saying Jan Brady doesn't have issues (get on the 70's sitcom bandwagon people!). Do you have anything that is weighing your heart down today? When I woke up this morning, I would have had a blank slate to create an amazing day. However, a past incident flooded my mind. It was a time when I hurt someone's feelings. Although I had worked through it, apologized and was forgiven, I relived every step, every word, and I was beating myself up for it again. Even though I knew that I handled it properly the first time around, my heart still felt heavy.

How about you? Do you have anything—big or small—that you're having a hard time letting go? List it out in your journal. When you look at what you wrote, are there any actions you can take to resolve the issues? If so, get on it. Do you need to ask for forgiveness from God and/or someone in particular? After you do, or if you already have done what is in your power, you'll be looking at a list that is weighing you down by your choice. Do you understand that you would be buying into the enemy's plan, being rendered useless or less effective by this false guilt you are feeling? So, what does God want us to do with that list?

Transformation by Truth

Therefore, since we are surrounded by such a great cloud of witnesses, let us throw off everything that hinders and the sin that so easily entangles, and let us run with perseverance the race marked out for us. (Hebrews 12:1)

Picture in your mind that you are wearing a backpack. Whatever you listed in your journal is a big, heavy rock. Even if you have only one rock, it'll quickly wear you down. By faith, take each of those rocks out one by one and let the issue go. Look at how God forgives:

(A)s far as the east is from the west,
so far has he removed our transgressions from us. (Psalm 103:12)

Let go of the heaviness so you can run with endurance the race God has set before you. Not only will you feel free and lighter, you will also have an amazing testimony for your cloud of witnesses. If God has removed your transgressions as far as the east is from the west, what gives you the authority to not follow God's lead? Do you think your standards are better than His? Do you think you can judge better than God?

Mind:

The greatest minds are capable of the greatest vices as well as of the greatest virtues. —Rene Descartes

When you are in a mind gridlock, like I was as I regretted yelling that I was the Kwanzaa lady, what does your inner dialogue sound like? For me, it sounded something like this, "*What* just came out of my mouth? I am a *fool*. How many people just heard that? Why can't I let things

Day 29

go? Was it really necessary for that woman to recognize me in the first place? Will I *ever* learn to keep my big mouth shut?!"

Yes, obsession is quite a vice for my mind. But here's the silver lining: it doesn't take much to transform my neurotic mind into a faith powerhouse. I obviously have the ability to focus on things; I just need to center that energy on things that are worthwhile. How can you change your inner dialogue into something productive instead of destructive? Or can you quiet the chatter altogether? Journal your findings.

Body:

I spent the first 28 years of my life obsessing about what I didn't like about my body. It wasn't curvy. Actually, that's not completely true. The one and only curve I seemed to have was under my belly button, and it was an outward curve. My arms were skinny; my legs were stocky for my height. I could go on and on about my unhealthy views of my body until I lived through my heart failure and survival. From that point on, I celebrated all the reasons I loved my body.

I quickly learned that my body is the most amazing gift to be marveled. My heart beats on its own. I can breathe without any conscious effort. And somehow, all the trillions of cells inside of me miraculously know what to do. Once I got my strength back, I sculpted my body to maximize my unique build. Now I can say with sincerity that I love my toned arms and strong, lean legs.

And guess what happened to the curve under my belly button? Absolutely nothing! It's still there. I have the body fat percentage of an athlete, yet I still have a pooch (not a dog reference). A nutritionist I once worked with explained that

I could get rid of it if I got my body fat down to 11 percent. That was the moment I realized I had to let it go.

While you are in the process of maximizing your body's potential, how can you make peace with your thighs, your excess curves or your lack of curves? What can you brag about? God purposely made your body wonderfully unique and beautiful. Are you appreciating his masterpiece? Journal those thoughts. Do what you can. Let go of the rest.

Day 30

I don't know about you, but in my family, we grew up with a lot of Mom and Dad-isms. You know what I'm talking about, right? My Mom raised us with the fear of going blind without proper lighting. Every time she walked into a dimly lit room where we were reading, she'd ask, "Are you going to night school?" A couple others from her repertoire were, "The world doesn't revolve around you." "Money doesn't grow on trees." Aye yai yai! That last one was my response; it wasn't another Mom-ism. Then there was my Dad. His sayings taught us to have a positive mindset, "Hang in there. The sun will rise again tomorrow." "There's a difference between playing to win and playing to not lose. Play to win and get aggressive!"

Learning to use the power of my mind through the Dad-isms has benefited me in numerous ways. Oddly enough though, his way of thinking made the hardest part of my life thus far even more difficult. My sister and I didn't grow up with our parents being spiritual leaders. So when they went through their heart-breaking battles against cancer, they valiantly fought with optimism more than crying out to God. Talking about death and dying was out of the question. Lori and I desperately wanted to pray with them or to be real about our sadness and fears. But in our parents' minds, that would have meant we were letting defeat creep into our home and that was unacceptable.

Mom was really on her decline. She had officially refused any further treatment for her cancer. Her eyes and skin were yellow from severe jaundice. It took all her strength to use her walker to move from one room to the next. Thankfully, my sister and I could be honest with each other. We knew her days were numbered. With tears in her eyes, Lori asked me if I knew how to make Mom's famous apple pie. This is the pie that was our Mom's outpouring of love at every family gathering. It wasn't her style to share her love through words or physical affection. Instead, it was by her pies that she celebrated victories, mended broken hearts and welcomed new friends. And believe me, there's not a pie on the face of this earth that can hold a candle to Margaret Sase's apple pie.

I told Lori that I had made it a few times, but it never tasted quite like Mom's. The crust was never as flakey and the apples came out too crunchy. It turned out she was in the same boat. So although we were afraid that our Mom and Dad would view our request as a sign of surrender, we asked our Mom if she would teach us to make her pie. "Maybe you could sit at the table and monitor what we do. You could give us directions like, 'Use more sugar' or, 'Roll the dough out thinner.' We don't want you to lift a finger. We will do all the work. Would this be possible?" With the sweetest hint of a smile, she agreed.

As I drove to our parents' home that day, I was already getting choked up. I knew this was the day that our Mom would unofficially hand us her legacy. I opened the front door and expected to find her in bed. To my surprise, her weak voice called me to the kitchen. I turned the corner to see a sight that will always bring tears to my eyes. She was sitting in a chair, her hair was brushed and you could tell she put time into looking beautiful. On the table in front of her were two perfectly-thought-out work stations. Both areas had mixing bowls and measuring spoons. Every needed ingredient was

Day 30

laid out with precise organization. The apples were already peeled and waiting to be sliced. This was obviously a monumental project which must have taken just about everything she had left to give.

I don't remember much about the conversation that day. I do remember learning all of the detailed touches that made our Mom's pie distinctly her own. Since then, my sister and I have made our Mom's pies for our family gatherings. For our uncles and grandma, those pies are more cherished than any gift we could ever buy. I have had the honor of teaching two of my closest friends how to make her signature recipe. With my Mom's pies, I realize that I'm feeding more than someone's sweet tooth. Instead, I'm feeding hearts with the legacy of my Mom's love.

APPLICATIONS

Heart:

You and I have a unique opportunity. We have the ability to create the legacy that we leave behind. I once heard a speaker who had been diagnosed with a terminal disease and was expected to live less than a year. She was a young, beautifully vibrant lady who had a five-year-old daughter. After researching the cognitive development of children, she came face-to-face with the fear that her daughter wouldn't be able to recall much about her Mommy after she died. Her mission from that moment on was to live and love on such a grand level that her little girl would remember distinct details of her Mommy. At the time, Sierra was also five years old and this testimony of truly living life to its fullest shook me to my core.

Transformation by Truth

Make a list of people who you impact on a regular basis. Next to their names, write a description of how you want their lives to be affected by your touch. Once you complete this exercise, go back to your personal mission statement. If you live out your mission each day, will that be enough to leave your one-of-a-kind fingerprint on the lives that surround you? If not, how can you alter your mission so it clearly reflects your legacy?

I'm no fortune teller (although some think I have played one on TV), but I will guess that when you dug in deep and wrote what you want your legacy to be, you didn't focus on money, possessions or status. I will guess you wrote more about relationships and how you were going to love based on actions, not feelings.

Be imitators of God, therefore, as dearly loved children and live a life of love, just as Christ loved us… (Ephesians 5:1-2)

Paul knew that walking in love makes our character Christ-like. It's a perfect response to the immeasurable gift of love we've been given from God Himself. And in doing so, we are creating the most impactful legacy imaginable.

Mind:

When Ryan and I first started dating, we went to a church where the pastor looked like a round Colonel Sanders. To start one of his sermons, he silently paced back and forth in front of the podium. We were all so quiet, you could have heard a pin drop. When he finally spoke, he looked intently at each of us as he posed this sobering question, "How many of you think you will make it out of this world alive?" There was a long pause as he continued to pace, "Really. Do any of you

Day 30

believe that you will make it out of this earthly world alive?" You could feel the unspoken tension in the room. He pointed his finger at us and said with conviction, "The moment you understand that you have an end-date here, *that* will be the moment you can truly live this life with authenticity and with godly purpose."

On the surface, it seemed like basic knowledge. Yep, I have an end-date. I was over it. Move on. Until... I got real with myself and realized that in my mind, I live as if time will go on forever just as it is now. When I look at my life today, much of the time I assume Sierra will always be a little wiggly, silly and chatty girl. I take for granted the health and strength Ryan and I enjoy each day. So, I am challenged to get that concept back in my mind. I have an end date here on earth and I have no idea when it is. I do know the legacy I want to leave behind, but it's easy to find myself thinking, "I just need to get my to-do list done, *then* I'll spend time impacting others' lives."

> *Show me, O LORD, my life's end*
> *and the number of my days;*
> *let me know how fleeting is my life.*
> *You have made my days a mere handbreadth;*
> *the span of my years is as nothing before you.*
> *Each man's life is but a breath. (Psalm 39:4-5)*

How are you going to, in the midst of your hectic life, remember that you are building your legacy? Your to-do list *is* life. I use index cards for my big life lessons and I place them on the dashboard of my car. One of my friends keeps his mission statement on a small card that he has in the front of his wallet. What is your tactic to remind yourself that you are building your legacy every moment of every day? How can you implement that idea, starting today, so your living legacy will be at the forefront of your mind? Journal your ideas and put them into action.

Body:

What will your physical legacy be? Will you be someone who takes such good care of your body that you'll be the feisty senior who plays hide-and-go-seek with the kids? Granted, I'm all for an age cut-off for hiding under the bed. No one wants to hear, "I've hidden and I can't get up!" Anyhow, back to my point. Can you be the role model who embraces your unique body—flaws and all? Can you be someone who teaches future generations that our "flaws" are actually beautiful and they make us wonderfully unique?

Think about the impact you can have on others by the way you live your life. What if you're already older now and you are in poor condition? What message would you give those around you if you decided to transform your health and fitness now? If you have *dis*abilities, how can you use your body to show God's *a*bilities? Imagine how your legacy could bless those who are facing similar struggles. All you need is a shift of perspective. Journal your legacy and enjoy living your story!

Now What?!

These Are a Few of my Favorite Things...

I hope you find joy and inspiration for your new healthy life in these resources... I know I did!

Books that helped me transform my faith...
Waking the Dead by John Eldredge
and
Crazy Love by Francis Chan

The one that taught me how to dream...
The Dream Giver by Bruce Wilkensen

The book that taught me to not conform any longer to the crazy patterns of this world...
Margin by Richard A. Swenson, M.D.

To renew and transform your mind...
Battlefield of the Mind by Joyce Meyer
and
Who Switched Off My Brain by Dr. Caroline Leaf

For natural healthy living...
The Seven Pillars of Health by Don Colbert, M.D.

To bring joy to eating while controlling mindless eating...
Press Pause Before You Eat by Dr. Linda Mintle

A book for those who are just starting their physical transformation...
Winning by Losing: Drop the Weight, Change Your Life by Jillian Michaels

For those of you who desire spiritual and emotional healing...
Hidden Joy in a Dark Corner: The Transforming Power of God's Story by Wendy Blight

The website I use for healthy inspiration, workouts, calorie tracking, discussion boards, recipes and more...
www.sparkpeople.com

To find a farmers market near you...
www.localharvest.org

The music that lights my heart on fire and brings God's truth to my soul...
Release by Ryan Dey

Appendix A

Let's Get This Workout Party Started!

Before you get rolling, it's wise to consult your physician for a thumb's up. Once you have the green light, schedule moderate to vigorous cardiovascular training (aerobic exercise) five days per week and strength training (resistance/weight training) on at least two of those five days. Well, that sounds good in theory, but do you know how to put it into action? Here are some ideas:

Gold Card Budget:

Hire a certified personal trainer for a month to create a customized a plan for your goals and to instruct you on proper form. If you hit a plateau or if you get bored, schedule another appointment for a tune-up. As you interview your potential trainers, consider asking these questions:

- What is your educational background and what credentials do you have?
- How can you best describe your energy level?
- Will your motivational technique be a good fit for my personality?
- How attentive are you with your clients? (Watch them as they are training someone else.)
- Do you have referrals who are my age and who have similar lifestyles and goals as I do?

Make sure they are not someone who will stick you on a treadmill by yourself as they do something else and count that as part of your paid session. If this is how they typically warm clients up, let it be known that you can come in five to ten minutes early and do this on your own before your session starts. You shouldn't be paying for that wasted time. This is an investment. Use your gold card wisely!

Debit Card Budget:

You can purchase a gym membership, but instead of hiring a trainer, you can take free group exercise classes. I, of course, am a bit biased since I love teaching classes and I also transformed my own body through group formats. You can mix it up between resistance classes and cardiovascular training. Keep things fresh by trying different types of classes such as dance, sculpting, spinning, kick boxing, water aerobics, boot camp and more. These usually have kickin' music, so it's high energy. If you arrive early to class, you can explain to the instructor that you are new. A great leader will help you set-up and get you acquainted with the workout. Another benefit that I didn't initially expect was meeting friends and gaining an added sense of accountability. The same people would look for me and ask me if I was okay when I didn't show up.

I Got $20 in My Pocket:

Download workouts online for your tablet computer or purchase DVD workouts. You can check out www.collagevideo.com. They have their workouts organized by goal type, intensity, style and instructors. You can read customers' comments and ratings and even view clips of the videos. I highly recommend having videos even if it's not your primary way to workout. We all have days when we are sequestered at home or when we travel. If you pack your tablet or laptop and your workout DVDs, you are set for your travels! You can even maintain your resistance workouts by downloading or purchasing a strength DVD that uses a resistance band (it won't take up much space in your suitcase and it's not heavy) and your own body weight as resistance. I usually travel with 2 DVD's: one that is pure cardio and one that is resistance training.

Hey... I Just Found Change in my Car:

Grab a hold of a fitness magazine. Most have workout plans included in each issue. Annual subscriptions are less than $2 per month. My friends and I each have a subscription and we trade them after we're done reading.

Someone Robbed my Piggy Bank:

You actually don't need any money if you have a dog. No doubt, you will have the cutest running or power walking partner in town. But, if you'd rather get out with a human, instead of gabbing on the phone, why not meet your friend for a power walk or jog and get lost in conversation for an hour? If you're a part of a Bible study group, dedicate part of your time together to exercise. Side note: you should be winded and should be speaking a few words at a time or you're not getting your heart rate up enough. Make sure you choose a partner who is as at least as dedicated as you, but preferably find someone who is even more dedicated. This is why dogs are great—they get into their new exercise habits quickly and they will use those puppy dog eyes to guilt you into each workout.

That will be your cardio workout. Now you'll just need to add strength training. For resistance training, you can Google "body resistance workouts" so you can strengthen your muscles without spending a dime.

You can also check out workout videos from your public library or search online for free workouts. There are many videos for both cardio and strength training.

Appendix B

Should I Count Calories, Points or my Blessings?

Always count your blessings! For the rest, here's the scoop. When you are in the process of losing weight, calories *do* count... whether they come in the form of calories or points. I tend to face a lot of opposition when I try to get someone to count theirs. I get it. So, my recommendation is this: if you clean up your eating and add in exercise and you are losing weight, fantastic. Keep doing what you're doing. Period.

But, if you're doing all that and your weight isn't budging, it's time to crunch some numbers. Your Basal Metabolic Rate (BMR) is how many calories your body needs to function each day. Basically, it's how many calories you need to sit in front of the TV all day long. You can use the calculation below, or you can Google "BMR calculator" and input your height, weight, age and select your gender. Do not add in any other information. When you click "calculate," you will get your BMR. But, for you math brainiacs, have fun with this equation!

Women: BMR = 655 + (4.35 x weight in pounds) + (4.7 x height in inches) - (4.7 x age in years)
Men: BMR = 66 + (6.23 x weight in pounds) + (12.7 x height in inches) - (6.8 x age in years)

Example: A 45-year-old female weighs 180 pounds and is 5'6". Her BMR equation would be:

655 + (4.35 x 180) + (4.7 x 66) − (4.7 x 45)
655 + 783 + 310 − 212 = 1536

Her BMR is 1536. That's how many calories her body burns if she is a couch potato. Once you figure out your *own* BMR, that will be a good amount of calories to eat per day in order to lose weight. If you are eating just enough calories to be inactive, your daily life (walking around the house, dropping the kids off at school, visiting work clients, etc.) plus your workouts will give you a calorie deficit. In other words, you will be expending more energy than what you are eating. Every time your calorie deficit equals 3500 calories, you just lost a pound.

So we start with a baseline calorie burn which is our BMR. In addition to that, we burn calories by our basic daily living, not including workouts. Here are very good approximates on how many calories your day-to-day activities burn:

10% of your BMR-	Mainly sedentary lifestyle such as a receptionist (in our example, that would burn an extra 153.6 calories per day)
20% of your BMR-	Somewhat active lifestyle such as an outside sales representative (our example would burn an extra 307.2 calories per day)
30% of your BMR-	Active lifestyle such as a personal trainer (our example would burn an extra 460.8 calories per day)
40% of your BMR-	Very active such as a construction worker (our example would burn an extra 614.4 calories per day)

Appendix B

Your workouts will give you a bigger calorie burn. You can either wear a heart rate monitor which tracks calories burned (this is very accurate), or you can use a website to estimate your calories burned by Googling "calories burned by exercise."

Going back to our example, let's say our 45-year-old female friend who weighs 180 pounds and is 5'6" ate 1536 calories per day. She's a sales representative so in her daily living she burns 307 calories per day. She tries out a 60 minute dance-based class at the gym and burns an additional 604 calories. This would give her a calorie deficit of 911. Since it takes a calorie deficit of 3500 calories to lose a pound, in 3.84 days of this eating and activity, she would lose one pound.

Appendix C

What Does it Mean to be a Christian?

What in the world do people mean when they say they are "born again"? It can sound a little wacky, eh? Those two words are referring to becoming a new creation by accepting that Jesus died for your sins. Jesus is God's precious and only Son. He was a living sacrifice for you and me. Jesus was without any sin but He took the weight of everyone's sin. He was crucified in a demeaning and horrific way. So when you receive this gift, all of your sins are forgiven because Jesus took your place in death—The weight of your sin was put on Jesus when He was crucified. As far as your sin is concerned, it has been removed from you as far as the east is from the west (Psalm 103:12). You are washed completely clean (1 Corinthians 6:11).

And this amazing love story doesn't end there. Jesus didn't just die for you, but God also raised Him up from death to life. You were in Jesus when He died, and you are in Jesus living a resurrected life. You are raised up to live a new life with a new heart. You'll have a new spirit because God puts *His* Spirit (the Holy Spirit) in you which will guide you in God's ways (Ezekiel 36:26-27). Why would Jesus do this? For the incomparable delight of giving you the opportunity to accept His gift, to live the most amazing life here and to be with Him throughout eternity. He loves you *that* much!

One of the many reasons I love the book of Romans is because it shows that there is NO WAY for us to be "good enough" to earn our way to heaven. In fact, we find that we fall way short all the time when we judge our actions and intentions against the "Law" that God gave Moses in the Old Testament. Do you ever feel like you were working so hard—to the point of exhaustion—but you still feel worthless since you keep on missing the mark? Well, wouldn't you say it's about time to drop out of that rat race? God is offering us an unimaginable gift—the gift of grace. God is saying that we can be made right, not by working to the bone, but by faith in the sacrifice of His one and only Son.

The simplest heartfelt conversation (prayer) with God is all you need to open that door to an amazing relationship; to live the most adventurous, incredible and purpose-filled life. Come into agreement with me by reading this simple but life-changing prayer aloud to receive Jesus into your heart and be born again:

Dear Heavenly Father,

Thank You for your overwhelming love. I know there is nothing I could possibly do to earn the salvation You offer through Your Son Jesus, but I humbly accept this gift You freely offer by Your grace. I believe that You love me dearly just the way I am, mistakes and all. I confess by speaking out loud that Jesus is my Lord and Savior. I know in my heart that Jesus died as a sacrifice for my sins and You raised Him from the dead. Thank you for forgiving all of my sins and reconciling me to You by this beautiful sacrifice. I am now a new creation and I am excited for this new, fresh start. I accept your love! In Jesus' name I pray, Amen.

If you just made this life-changing decision, please let a Christian know! They will want to celebrate with you and

Appendix C

walk with you through this journey. Remember, there are no silly questions. We all have them. Have the courage to share them and get to know our God more intimately through them.

Made in the USA
Lexington, KY
04 May 2015